THE HUMAN ADVENTURE

A Study Course for Christians on Sexuality

Robert J. L. Matthews

THE HUMAN ADVENTURE

Copyright © 1980 by
The C.S.S. Publishing Company, Inc.
Lima, Ohio

All rights reserved. No portion of this book may be reproduced or utilized in any form or by any means, electronic or mechanical including photocopying, without permission in writing from the publisher. Inquiries should be addressed to: The C.S.S. Publishing Company, Inc., 628 South Main Street, Lima, Ohio 45804.

ISBN 0-89536-426-3   PRINTED IN U.S.A.

TABLE OF CONTENTS

Acknowledgments	5
Foreword	7
Introduction	12
1. **Historical Background**	15
2. **Biblical Background**	35
3. **Contemporary Theories of Sexuality**	53
Sex as Pleasure	53
Sex as Religion	55
Sex and Idealism	58
Sex as Hot or Cool	63
Sex and Theology	67
4. **Male-Female Differences**	71
What Are the Specifics of the Problem?	72
The Various Women's Organizations	76
How Are Men Reacting?	77
Do Men Have Problems Too?	78
What Are the Facts about Male-Female Differences?	83
Differences in General	87
What About Sexual Differences?	90
Some Further Thoughts about Male-Female Differences	96
5. **Pre-Marital Sexuality**	99
The Social Situation	100
The Bible and Pre-Marital Sexuality	103
The Sacramental View	105
Some Contemporary Views	107
Humanists	107
Situation Ethics or the New Morality	108
The Social Sciences	109

    A New Look at Virginity 111

6. Homosexuality 121
    What is Homosexuality? 126

7. Marriage 137
    Some Quotes from the Marriage Critics 137
    The Alternatives to Marriage 140
        Open Marriage 140
        Adultery 141
        Contract Cohabitation 142
        Serial Monogamy (Divorce) 144
        Group Sex 145
        Casual Sex 146
    In Defense of Traditional Monogamy 147
        Indissolubility 148
        Freedom 150
        Adultery 154
        Fidelity 156

Afterword 158

Bibliography 159

ACKNOWLEDGMENTS

Many people deserve thanks for their help in the writing of this book. The members of the original discussion group who were brave enough to try out the whole idea were most helpful with their support, suggestions, and honest, creative participation, whether positive or negative. They are: Sally Casad, Elaine Creaden, Nancy K. Hanson, Mr. Dennis Helm, Mary Louise Hurlbut, Gordon Hurlbut, Kent Kalb, Blanche Matthews, Betty M. Nelick, Claire Sutton, Max Sutton, Mrs. Linda C. Swartz, Lillian Thomas, Mrs. Rita Tracy, and JoAnne Wright.

My brother, the Rev. Daniel P. Matthews, and sister-in-law, Diane Vigeant Matthews, facilitated the whole process greatly by inviting me to give two seminars on this subject in their church.

My wife's brother, the Rev. Dr. John P. Davis, whose sudden death at forty-three was a tragic loss, and his wife, Mary Dee Davis, studied the manuscript and commented in very helpful detail with many suggestions, most of which were gratefully incorporated.

The Rev. John Paschall Davis, whose death occurred just after the book was finished, and his wife, Evelyn Ames Davis (my father- and mother-in-law) were most helpful in reviewing the manuscript and suggesting many astute stylistic changes.

Particular thanks are due to the Rev. Dr. Kenneth R. Mitchell whose help was invaluable in many ways, particularly in clearing up internal inconsistencies and placing the whole work in a more helpful context.

Thanks are due to a very able typist, Joan Moore, and Sandra S. Wiechert for excellent editing.

To our sons, Robert, John, and Paul, go thanks for their gracious acceptance of fatherly neglect during a summer spent in writing.

Most of all I am indebted to my wife, Blanche, who has influenced me more than anyone else in this as in every other subject. Her literary editing as well as theological insight have been invaluable. Beyond all such practical help, it has been our relationship that has given reality to the theories about sexuality being the God-given structure through which he works most powerfully. For that I will always be grateful to her and to God.

Robert Matthews
St. Matthias Day, 1978
Lawrence, Kansas

FOREWORD

Formal study of sexuality came rather late in my life. It was during the first seven years in the ministry, with its heavy demands for marital counselling, that I became convinced that I had a lot to learn about sex. So I left the parish and went to the Menninger Foundation in Topeka, Kansas, for a year's training course for clergy in the wisdom of psychiatry. There I started to remedy my ignorance. But it was just a start. As all good education does, it trains you in how to explore the subject for the rest of your life. This study course for Christian adults is my latest effort in that continuing process.

The primary effort here has been to pull together some insights about sexuality that come from the two disciplines of psychology and theology. I have made little attempt to separate these two sources since I believe that God is involved in any honest search for truth about anything, whether its object is the Deity or human sexuality.

The intended setting for this study course is a small (8 to 12), informal discussion group of adult men and women within a parish family. The structure is for the participants to commit themselves to seven weekly discussion sessions lasting about one and one-half hours each with a chapter to read before each discussion. Through experience with such groups it has seemed that seven weeks is a possible period of time to expect busy people to commit themselves. For this reason the topics for study have been limited to what the author has arbitrarily decided were the most important. Ideally the person designated as the leader should have some professional competence in sexuality and group process. But since such a person will often not be available, the reading material has been purposefully designed to help keep the discussion objective and educational rather than subjective and therapeutic. With that goal in mind, anyone with good leadership qualities should be able to fulfill the role of leader. No questions for discussion have been added to the ends of the chapters because the author feels that such questions are often seen as an insult to the capacity of adults for dealing with the topics on their own. But if thought helpful, the leader might prepare his/her own such questions for use as discussion starters.

It is my belief that learning for adults takes place most effectively in a small, informal group discussion with some "content" material having been assimilated before the discussion. In this setting a variety of opinions is encouraged. The goal is not agreement but rather the comparison of beliefs and experiences. It is during the quiet reflection after the discussion that true education or growth takes place. That kind of change can happen most easily in the privacy of one's own thoughts. The discussion needs to contain, therefore, as many various opinions as possible. The average adult usually holds more than one position on almost every subject. But because we all want to appear consistent, we usually admit to only one view. A major purpose in writing the material the way I have is to present to the participants various views of human sexuality. The hope is that, in reading views other than the ones with which the reader is most compatible, some help is given for the participant to recognize conflicting views within him/herself and thus learn first of all more about his/her own complexity. If one is able to accept the variety within one's self, it is much easier to live with the conflicting views of others and also to understand their ambivalences. It is my belief that good group discussion must struggle with opposing views. It is out of the tensions created by differing versions of the "truth" that a deeper, more complex, and yet possibly more comprehensive "truth" can be found. The reading material is designed to stimulate such discussion by presenting differing views with little editorial comment. After the various views have been presented, the author does not avoid presenting his own opinions, but usually these are not intruded early, and are hopefully a contribution to the resolution of the conflicts which might have arisen.

A group discussion leader has the job of facilitating the dialogue or "enabling" the various conflicting views to be presented in an accepting and non-judgmental atmosphere. The group leader needs to be secure enough to present some of his/her own confusions or ambiguities about a topic if other members of the group are not forthcoming with their own. The leader needs always to be aware of when he/she has to play the "devil's advocate" (which implies he/she would defend views which he/she may usually oppose) in order to stimulate the discussion.

The leader's second responsibility is to be aware of the need to do the opposite of creating controversy: to contribute to harmony, understanding, and unity within the group when this is not being accomplished by other group members. If all of us hold within ourselves differing views about many aspects of our subject, so the group needs to be able to come to some acceptance of difference and conflict within a more comprehensive loyalty and acceptance of the value of the group itself.

The third role of the leader is to help people talk who do not do it easily, and to keep others from talking too much when they tend to dominate the group.

With these three jobs in mind at all times, the leader has a difficult role to play. But he/she should not be so determined to fulfill the leader's role that he/she fails to be a participant in the discussion as well. The ideal group leader envisioned for this course is one who is as involved in the discussion as anyone else, but who from time to time leaves the role of just another participant to observe the process and react appropriately if it is necessary to fulfill any of the three obligations mentioned above.

My own position on this subject is never completely set forth in any one place in the reading material. The reason for this is that I do not intend to stimulate very much discussion in the group about the views of the absent author. I would rather have as little time as possible be spent discussing my beliefs. Instead, I hope that my opinions have been included in ways that will make it as easy as possible for the participants to react to them either negatively or positively in the process of presenting their own views.

Briefly my position is this: Our culture is in a sexual crisis. It may not be a revolution because that implies more radical change in sexual activity than is probably occurring. But a crisis, or decisive moment, it seems to be. Medically, the word crisis means the change in a disease which indicates whether the result is to be recovery or death. I think our society is sexually sick, and it seems as if we have reached the crisis of this illness. But which way the crisis is going to go we cannot tell. We could be on the verge of a new and more healthful sexual maturity. Maybe we are entering a sexual renaissance. But we could just as easily be heading for a "dark age" for human sexuality.

The church has been a major source of the beliefs and ideals about sexuality held by Western society. There are contained within the history of this development both the ideals which can still be useful in fashioning a new understanding of sexuality, and the problems that to a great extent have led to our present sexual malaise. We need to explore and understand both of these.

The Christian faith is belief in a God who loves. The Incarnation is the fundamental expression of that love. God used a body to love us. For Christians, therefore, the love of God is to be best understood and received as mediated through a body. Humans created in God's image are given bodies through which to love in the same way God loves. People come in two different bodily forms which are designed to need each other. Therefore, the study of sexuality is one of the most practical applications of the discipline of theology. To know how God and human beings are related is to have great insight into the way one half of the human race ought to be relating to the other half.

I believe a sexual renaissance is possible. It might be helped to take place if enough Christians struggle together in a sincere attempt to:
1. Understand more deeply their own sexuality.
2. Become knowledgeable about the problem in our society.
3. Search for their understanding of God's will for them in these matters.

This would obviously result in some action. What form that action would take is impossible to foresee since renaissances are notoriously unpredictable, and so are God's ways of getting his will accomplished.

Hopefully this study course can contribute in a small way toward preparing its participants to respond to the role God may give them in what we hope is his coming Sexual Renaissance.

INTRODUCTION

What is human sexuality? It may seem ridiculous to begin this study with such a question. It is like asking, "What is a person?" You either know because you are one, or there is no sense in asking because you are not. Sexuality is something we all experience as part of ourselves. The very fact that we exist means we are sexual beings. Sexuality is not an optional part of life.

Having agreed on that, we admit that it may be the last thing on which we are all going to agree concerning this subject! Sex is a mystery — a very great mystery. Freud seemed to give the impression that he knew a lot about it, but the best he could do was to give us some mythology about Libido, and Eros, and "tension-states," and Oedipal Conflicts. But, of course, that is exactly what we needed. Myths and symbols are the best tools to use when we tinker with a mystery. Even when we are finished, the result is usually more mystery, not less.

If sexuality were only a problem, we could get on with discovering the solution, because problems are manageable; mysteries are not. There are certain aspects of sexuality which we could consider as problems; for instance, how best to express it under certain circumstances. These problems, however, are always found embedded in the greater mystery of sexuality itself. So, while sexuality presents us with many knotty problems, it will also continue to haunt us by its mystery.

Sexuality always faces us with the known and the unknown simultaneously, and has in this regard an impact on us similar to that of religion, which has as its subject the knowable and yet unknowable God. Sexuality also tends to lure us seductively into even greater mysteries than itself. We cannot flirt seriously with sex without also becoming involved with questions about ultimate meaning and value. Sex and religion always wind up hand in hand if we allow them enough freedom to choose their partners.

1
Historical Background

There exists a very common, popular mythological version of the historical beginnings of sexuality. William Cole has given us his version of it in this way: The first human beings were natural. They had no hang-ups about sex. They walked naked and unashamed in the first garden of Eden. They were carefree and totally without guilt in their state of perfect sexual freedom. Then came Christianity, disguised as a serpent. It convinced these beautiful, innocent people that their bodies were evil and disgusting, that they should cover their nakedness and begin to discipline their sexual urges. To give up sex completely would have been the Christian ideal, but the church had to settle for something less since even Christianity had to adjust to the fact that the race had to be perpetuated. At least Christianity was successful forever after in making people feel guilty about sex.[1]

Is it not sad that we were not all born before the guilt hit, back in those carefree garden of Eden days when everything was fun? Of course, that is pure mythology, and a very ignorant form of myth at that. A brief look at the real world through history explains things quite differently. The facts are these.

Historically, there are two attitudes that have greatly affected our Western understanding of sex. The first is naturalism, which takes a positive, accepting attitude toward the physical, natural world. The second is dualism, which believes that everything physical or material is either illusory or evil, or both. In dualism, the realm of the spiritual is the only real one.

Classical Greek civilization was basically

naturalistic. Moderation was the highest good. This attitude prevailed from ca. 800 B.C. to Aristotle, who died in 322 B.C. The celibate as well as the libertine were equally condemned. Sin was not being moderate in all things, even virtue. Keeping all things in balance was the goal. In the fourth century B.C., however, the Alexandrian Empire allowed a new spirit to enter Greek thought. While Alexander believed he was the great missionary of the Greek genius to the backward East, the influence really flowed both ways. Oriental thought infected the Greeks, which meant an infusion of dualism. This created the culture of the Hellenistic Age with its highest good no longer moderation, but detachment, freedom from passion. Sex was regarded as low and degrading, an act in which humans descended to the level of the beast. Contrary to the myth, we see that the truth is that Western humanity had "fallen" long before Christianity arose.

After Greece came Rome. Before the fifth century B.C., few persons were more powerful in their own world than the Roman patriarchs. A patriarch could kill or sell into slavery members of his own family. He was the high priest in the worship of family ancestors. His wife's dowry was completely in his power and he could control all her actions because legally she was always considered a minor. As the state grew, it absorbed some of the father's power. During the Punic Wars (third century B.C.), the wives ran the farms and brought pressure on the Senate to change the laws. After that, women could marry without losing their own property. They became wealthy, but they still possessed no political rights. Many wealthy women turned to adultery as a means of expressing their individuality. Many men felt that women's freedom was responsible for the decaying morality.[2] The elder Cato said, "All men rule over women, we Romans rule over all men, and our wives rule over us."[3]

Roman religion strongly encouraged sexual activity. The god Virginiensis had the job of loosening the bride's girdle, the god Subigus saw to it that the bride yielded and the god Prema held her down while the man penetrated. Interestingly, there was no female god to ensure that the man did his part! Ovid, in his famous works on sexual techniques, says little about emotional involvement. Prostitution was very common during imperial times. Many of these women waited in the archways under public theaters and circuses after erotically stimulating shows. The Latin word for arches, "fornix," has given us the word fornication.

As Rome slowly crumbled, its moral corruption was replaced by a new concept of sexuality which the legions of Christ spread over the Empire. Judaism, out of which Christianity was born, had a naturalistic tradition. The church fought several battles during its early years to keep from being cut off from that healthy naturalism. Because the Incarnation is at the heart of Christianity, there should never be within it a rejection of the natural. Sadly enough, however, the one area of early Christian thinking that did become contaminated with dualism was its interpretation of sex.

The reason Christianity rejected sexuality in its early years is quite obvious. Poverty, unemployment, civil wars, plagues, pillage by barbarians, declining commerce, and a breakdown in the family, were all explained as the result of God's anger against the sensuality of the wealthy Romans. Also, the continual persecution of Christians produced many martyrs which encouraged the church to teach a form of piety that renounced the material world. Asceticism became the way to holiness. The body in all its aspects was to be fought against. Even to clean it was to give it too much attention. Baths were shunned. Simon Stylites, who died in A.D. 459, was one of the more amazing ascetics. He lived on the top of a pillar, bound with ropes caked with filth. He exemplified the ideal when he tenderly picked up a maggot that fell from his festering side and said, "Eat what God hath given you." Jerome said that a full-grown virgin should never bathe. She should be ashamed to see her own nakedness.

During the first five or six centuries of the Christian era, asceticism was the prevailing mood. Perfection was gained through renunciation of the world and subjection of the body, which always meant sexual continence. This was regarded by both Athanasius and Ambrose as a new and distinctively Christian virtue, yet the Church Fathers did not yield to the complete dualism which denounced marriage as an evil. Jerome came close when he praised marriage solely because it produces virgins. He also wrote:

> I do not condemn wedlock. Indeed (and this I say to make my meaning quite clear), I should like everyone to take a wife who cannot manage to sleep alone because he gets frightened at night.

Jerome is a great source of quotes from this age of Christian asceticism. He said a man should not love his wife with passion but with judgment. In fact, he said, he who loved his wife too ardently was no more than an adulterer. A church council in A.D. 398 pronounced that out of reverence for the priestly blessing given at the end of the marriage ceremony, newlyweds should abstain from sexual union on the first night. But there was a way out: paying a moderate fee for a dispensation.

Clement of Alexandria was more creative when he wrote that marriage offers better opportunities than virginity for the attainment of excellence, involving as it does greater temptations and cares, and therefore more occasions for the exercise of self-discipline.

The most amazing form of sexual asceticism in the early church was known as "spiritual marriage." This meant the co-existence of the sexes in strict continence, though they might share the same house, room, or even bed. A Biblical allusion to this practice can be found in 1 Corinthians 7:36-38, which may indicate that it was attempted very early in Christian history.

In the year A.D. 385, the Pope tried to put celibacy on the books as a necessary requirement for clergy, but heavy opposition defeated this until 1215 when it was finally officially adopted.

It is difficult to explain this early Christian attitude toward things sexual. There was the common idea that to be sincere in the quest for the good life meant primarily renunciation. To be good was basically to avoid doing certain things. Another explanation might be that reason was understood as the highest function of the human personality. In sexual passion, reason was eclipsed by emotion and was therefore a dangerous experience. With that sort of outlook, sexuality made one less than human; therefore, it was degrading and sinful.

We must not, however, exclude the effect of the purely personal experience of very important people of that age. Augustine was such a one. His life story explains his theology more clearly than anything else. He was born in 354 and was a man of his age in the total sense. He passed through all the major beliefs of his time before his conversion to Christianity. As a Manichaean, he was taught a sweeping dualism which said the whole world was a battleground between the two cosmic forces of good and evil. The body was identified with the evil and the soul with the good. Augustine thought he ought to be able to be celibate, but he had a concubine, and found it impossible to break out of the prison house of the flesh. His prayer at that time was, "Give me chastity — but not yet." At thirty, his mother decided that marriage would help, so one was arranged. His concubine, after fifteen years of faithfulness on both their parts, was sent off, swearing eternal fidelity. Since his proposed bride was under age and Augustine had to wait for two years before he could marry her, he took a new mistress. It was during this time that due to the preaching of Ambrose, he began reading the Scriptures, and while studying Romans, heard the voice of God speaking directly to him. His conversion took away his lust, and Augustine felt able to become a celibate. It was a decision against both marriage and intercourse. His subsequent theology emerges directly out of his sexual struggles. He could not believe that sex was innately bad. It was a gift of God; he found the problem in concupiscence. This is the destructive impulse which drives a person toward the quest for self-satisfaction. It all began, according to Augustine, in Adam and Eve's Fall. Their pride and self-will got them into trouble. The act of rebellion against God made them conscious of a new and destructive impulse within themselves. Augustine called it lust. It affects all of life. It is the drive to seek meaning and purpose in oneself, or in what one can create. Its chief characteristic is instability, because the more a person gets in life, the more he wants, since nothing he gets truly satisfies. Nothing can take the place of God in a person's life, but if he does not know this then the quest for substitutes dominates his life. This lust, or concupiscence, affects all areas of life, but particularly the sexual, where human beings most easily act "irrationally." There is great inability of the will to govern the genitals. At one time tumescence occurs involuntarily, while at another, impotence makes the will useless.

For Augustine this meant that lust and original sin were almost the same thing. Adam and Eve might have been able to have intercourse before the Fall without the emotional disturbance and loss of control, but after their rebellion they were no longer living in full harmony with reason and nature. And the punishment was not to be able to have control of all their own faculties. Their disobedience to God resulted in disobedience to the self, symbolized and made concrete in their bodies. They still had control of their arms and legs, but their sexual organs seemed to have minds of their own. Sex lay beyond their control. This, then, is seen by Augustine as God's punishment for man's disobedience; man's body becomes disobedient to man. Since no sexual union takes place without this corrupting effect, which is both the result of sin and the punishment for it, intercourse becomes the way this problem is passed from parents to the next generation. It is easy to see why for Augustine Christ's virginal birth is so important. Since no lust was involved in his conception, he was free from sin.

For the fifth century Church, Hellenistic dualism had won a profound victory over Hebraic naturalism. Sexuality was thought of as something which threw the personality out of balance and was also seriously evil. During this period of history, there was no allowance for a personal love relationship within sexuality. It was a narrow, impersonal thing.

During the Middle Ages the theology of the Church concerning sexuality did not change in any major way. But much of its structure was more clearly defined. Up to the tenth century, marriages were performed by laymen in the home and in the eleventh and twelfth centuries in front of the Church; only later did marriage gradually pass into the hands of the priests.[4] With the ascent of the Christian emperors, the bishop, on invitation, was entitled to hear marriage cases. By the eleventh century, Pope Gregory VII was granted formal recognition from William the Conqueror of the church's right to try all matters pertaining to the "soul." By the twelfth and thirteenth centuries, the "soul" was interpreted to include the deadly sins of fornication, adultery, and the like. Abstinence was a favorite topic among theologians. One drew up a list of days on which intercourse should not take place. It included all the seasons of fasting and important festivals: Thursdays to commemorate the arrest of Jesus, Fridays to honor his death, Sundays in remembrance of the resurrection. Mary was given Saturday, and Monday was reserved to commemorate the deceased. This left for copulation only a few scattered Tuesdays and Wednesdays that did not fall on fast or feast days.[5]

When all this seemed about to threaten marriage, a liberal advanced the radical idea that lawful intercourse was actually meritorious. This liberal wing was supported by Thomas Aquinas who said that coitus was not in itself sinful. The difference from Augustine was in the fact that Augustine saw the sin of the Fall resulting in a compulsive desire for self-satisfaction that shows up most easily in sexuality. Aquinas saw the sin as producing only a near loss of the powers of concentration. For him, the great sensual pleasure that comes from intercourse is good. It is only the loss of control and reason that Aquinas finds sinful. But he still greatly preferred the state of virginity. He thought that marriage should receive a "goodness" value of 30; widowhood, 60; and virginity, 100. The married Christian could never attain the heights of the cleric because the cleric, in avoiding lust, retained his marvelous faculty of reason. Aquinas believed that the excessive lust which infects all sexual relations would not have been true in

Paradise (before the Fall) where the lower powers were entirely subject to reason. He held this belief so strongly that he was convinced that Adam and Eve could have determined the sex of their children by a mere act of will (!).

Aquinas did not agree with the concept that all pleasure is evil. For him there were good pleasures and bad pleasures. Pleasures were evil only when the things that produced them were contrary to reason and the will of God. Aquinas warned women against make-up or clothing that was designed to incite men's lust. According to him, it was permissible for a married woman to do so to please her husband, but unmarried women could not adorn or paint themselves without sin. Aquinas regarded marriage as a remedy for sin. He called it a medicine for immorality. In general, Aquinas followed Augustine's interpretation for sex and marriage, but with less suspicion of bodily pleasure. An interesting illustration of this is seen in his attitude toward intercourse between an engaged couple. He said, "In the judgment of the church, carnal intercourse following a betrothal is declared to make a marriage." (*Summa* Part 3, Q. 46, A. 2)[6] In God's sight they are married if the inner intention is for a true union. He believed that the ministers of the sacrament of marriage are the bride and groom themselves and the form of the sacrament is their reciprocal consent. This is still the fundamental Christian definition.

Prostitution was always denounced, and yet along with that condemnation went the idea that the present condition of human society made prostitution a necessary evil. Harlots were grudgingly seen as indispensable to the well-being of society. Aquinas said that prostitution was like the sewer in a palace. Take away the sewer and the palace will be filled with pollution.' This attitude is typical of the ambivalence of medieval sexual thought. Here the church is giving a semblance of approval to a double standard of morality which the New Testament and the early Fathers had condemned.

An old problem with a new look that arose during the Middle Ages was the image of woman as temptress. Novella d'Andrea (1312-1366) was one of the few learned women admitted to a chair in the venerable University of Bologna. But when she lectured, it was from behind a curtain lest her face should distract the students.[8]

This caricature of woman as the potential ruin of man reaches its height in the medieval theory of witchcraft. In 1486 the book *Witches' Hammer (Malleus Maleficarum)* was issued by the Dominican inquisitors. It was a manual for detecting and prosecuting witches. The leading scholars of the church, from Aquinas down, accepted the belief that demons could and did cohabit with humans, especially women. Nor did any Protestant reformer utter a word against this theory. As late as 1768, John Wesley declared that "giving up witch-craft was giving up the Bible."[9]

This infamous book went through thirteen editions in thirty-four years and each time collected more evidence extracted from helpless women who under torture confessed everything that the imagination of the persecutors could suggest. The author's description of the feminine personality reaches a low which has never been equalled. Even the Latin word for women, *femina,* is derived from *fe* and *minus,* that is, "less in faith." According to *Witches' Hammer,* deceit is the very essence of woman's nature because she was formed from Adam's rib which was crooked.[10]

A fascinating fact is that this period in the twelfth and thirteenth centuries, with its systematic persecution of witches, also produced another phenomenon connected with sexuality — courtly love. It was certainly an ambivalent age. Along with the degrading of woman comes its opposite: putting her on a pedestal. This happened in the secular sphere. Its equivalent in religion was the beginning of mariology. The doctrine that Mary was immaculately conceived began to be formulated. It meant that Mary was conceived in the normal way, but without sin, meaning without the temporary suspension of reason of which all ordinary intercourse could be accused. This meant that Mary, a woman, could be morally sinless like Jesus. This made it possible to think of woman as possessing a dignity fully equal to that of man. Woman could therefore be an object of spiritual love, which is what courtly love was all about. The new doctrine also implied that there can be such a thing as a sinless act of sexual intercourse. It can be fully moralized and spiritualized.[11]

At the same time the greatest love affair of the Middle Ages added even more to the gradual acceptance of not only women in general, but women and their sexual natures as well. Abelard and Heloise were the "beautiful people" of their age. He was a lay theologian and philosopher who had everything. Heloise was beautiful, intelligent, devout, faithful, and also sensuous. The details of their romance are not as significant as is the lasting effect their story had on society. Heloise became pregnant before their secret marriage which was chosen as a solution in order not to hurt his reputation. After word of the marriage had leaked out, Heloise denied that she was married, again in an attempt to save Abelard's reputation. In anger, her uncle had Abelard castrated. She fled to a nunnery. Abelard found the shame even worse than the pain, and ordered Heloise to become a nun. Subsequent to her obedience, he would become a monk. This they did, in that order. Abelard's life after that was a sad anticlimax. Heloise, however, became a prioress and was much beloved by the church and her nuns. She was a model churchwoman, true to her vow of chastity, and yet what did her life say to the average person? It was probably this: If such a great woman has sexual desires, can sex really be evil? Is sensuality really incompatible with other virtues? Heloise gave society and the church a new model. Here was a pious woman who did not shun sexuality.

But more about the secular movement, courtly love. This great experiment was entered into by a relatively small number of late medieval aristocrats who dared to invent a whole new form of sexual interaction. What they tried to do was to make sexual feeling and behavior more personal. They wanted to bring conscious intention and control into the sexual realm and indeed dominate that basic human drive and make it serve the purposes of love. That sounds rather ordinary to us today, but at that time love and sex were thought to be incompatible entities. It was thought that the genital drive in its original state is not linked with human intentions. These revolutionaries thought they could do just that. But it required a learning process. Courtly lovers abstained, therefore, from all those aspects of sexual interaction that they could not bring within the range of personal intention and voluntary control. This "pure" love referred to the union of the hearts and minds of lovers who experience everything together except orgasm. This "pure" love is inexhaustible, because it continually increases tension without satisfying it. According to the code, love in marriage is impossible because true love thrives on freedom of choice. Courtly love is not the fulfillment of a contract but rather is spontaneous. By abstaining from orgasm, these sexual revolutionaries lengthened the period of personal-sexual intimacy. They created many new forms of sexual interest and expression. This broke the power of instinctual sexuality. Today this might be understood as the sublimating of sexuality. It was sublimated into the new art of "conversation." The new self-consciousness about their own feelings was heightened by the demand to communicate these feelings. Within the tradition of courtly love, the essence of love was understood to be this joining of two souls in an intimate union of mutual understanding and affection that was created by the power of speech alone. That is why kissing was considered such a significant act. Genital union was thought of as only uniting bodies, but kissing was uniting that part of the body that is the organ of the soul.[12]

Women achieved a new status through the doctrines of courtly love. It was the exaltation of the feminine. And this caused contradictory feelings in men — mistrust and terror (maybe witch hunts came from this), but also fascination and passion. It did compensate for the traditional inferior position of women. But in actuality it was mostly a new theory. There was not much real practice. This hothouse plant of a literary and worldly civilization could not ripen outside the aristocratic circle. When that social structure degenerated, all that was left was a literary convention.[13]

The sixteenth and seventeenth centuries produced a continued improvement in the status of women. The liberals of the time sought to increase the opportunities for women to realize some of their potential, beyond maternity, without infringing on the traditional rights of men. But the liberals were not the majority. John Knox was appalled that three countries, France, England, and Scotland, had women either governing or playing prominent roles of authority. He wrote:

> To promote a Woman to bear rule, superiority, dominion, or empire above any realm, nation, or city, is repugnant to Nature; contumely to God.

The reformers were not so radical in their views of sexuality as they were in other matters. Luther, being a former monk, demanded of everyone, not just clergy, the higher righteousness of poverty, chastity, and obedience. Chastity meant for him the proper use of sexuality, not its denial. Luther felt that two contemporary evils had to be eradicated. One was the licentiousness of the clergy. The solution for that was to encourage marriage for all and to attack the concept that God liked virgins best. The second was the right of the church to regulate marriage. Luther believed that marriage was not a sacrament since the Bible does not say that any special grace is given by God to married people. Also, he noted, marriage is of ancient origin and therefore could not be the possession of the church. He felt that intercourse was never without sin; but God excused it by his grace because the estate of marriage is his work and he preserves in and through the sin all that good which he has implanted and blessed in marriage. He said marriage may be likened to a hospital for incurables which prevents inmates from falling into a graver sin.[14]

Calvin affirmed sex and marriage as facts of creation. His predecessors had all looked upon woman as primarily a sexual being and upon marriage as principally for purposes of procreation. Calvin, however, was different. For him, the first aspect of marriage comes from the Biblical words, "It is not good that the man should be alone." It is first relational. Sex is subservient to community. John Milton, the English puritan, following Calvin's lead, recognized that loneliness is the first thing in Scripture that God says is not good.[15] When Calvin passed the age of thirty, he decided to marry, since he had so criticized Catholic clergy for their celibacy. Also, he wanted someone to free him from cares so that he could devote himself completely to God. His ideal was "chaste, agreeable, modest, frugal, patient, and affords me some hope that she will be solicitous for my personal health and prosperity." He found one in the widow Idelette de Bure. When she died a few years later he gave her the supreme compliment: she had never interfered with his work.[16] Calvin obviously had a greater appreciation for women than any previous theologian. For him she was no longer chained to her role as baby factory or safety valve for male libido.

During this period the Roman Catholic position on divorce did not change: neither divorce nor remarriage was possible while one spouse was living. Separation from bed and board was allowable. This stance was unanimously rejected by the Protestant Reformers. And yet divorce was not to be easily granted. Luther did not think that chronic marital bickering was a justification for divorce; separation maybe, but not divorce. As long as a man can have his spouse in bed, he cannot complain about her incessant nagging, for "he who wants a fire must endure the smoke." The majority of the divines of the sixteenth century were of the opinion that adultery dissolves the matrimonial bond, and that the remarriage of the innocent husband (some added the innocent wife too) is permissible. They believed this action to be based on Scripture (Matthew 19:9).[17]

From the Reformation to the present, it is difficult to trace changes in the Christian understanding of sexuality because of the proliferation of churches with various doctrines. It is also true that the major changes in people's understanding of this aspect of their nature begin to come during this period from secular sources rather than religious ones.

Romanticism is the next major movement. It had no connections with the church and developed primarily from literary sources. Wordsworth was against too much civilization; Coleridge fought against the tyranny of reason; Byron, middle class respectability; and Shelley, the evils of society. They all worshiped what they thought was natural to humans and that which was individually unique in each person. They all glorified sensation and emotion, and loved contrasts, oppositions, and antitheses. Romanticism was in many ways like courtly love. But there was one great difference. The Romantic was for open rebellion against the mores of the time. The courtly lover valued discretion. The Romantic did not bother to take so much time in expressing his/her love. He/she did not have to go through all the courtship stages of the courtly lover. The courtly lover was also happy and optimistic. The Romantic worshiped death because it represented total fusion with all of nature. Although it carried emotionalism to excess, romanticism fostered the idea of a natural relationship between the sexes. The acceptance of each individual for what he/she was, reflected a more egalitarian spirit than the rigid class distinctions of the past. Romanticism's basic ideas of equality helped to foster the dreams of the middle class, and its idealizing of the love relationship, subtly introduced the concept of woman as both a worthy person and an object of desire, since a man could not truly love an inferior person.[18]

Sigmund Freud, who died in 1939, is the last stop in this sketchy tour of the historical background of our subject. He was a non-practicing Jew who thought religion was an elaborate kind of wish fulfillment, or to be more technical: mass obsessional neurosis. His own marriage was very patriarchal, and certainly no positive example of any marriage ideals except fidelity. And yet, what he did in the establishment of the art of psychoanalysis radically changed the world's understanding of sexuality.

Freud possessed a fair amount of romantic passion for his wife-to-be. During their four year engagement he wrote over nine hundred letters to Martha Bernays. He was intensely jealous and had a compulsive need for perfection. When Freud's theories first came to public attention, he was considered a sex fiend. He was actually very traditional and naive in respect to women and personally rather prudish. He forbade his fiancee to skate since it would necessitate her holding another man's hand. Only after he learned that it was possible for a woman to skate unattended did he grant her permission to do so. He has often been called by experts one of the profound moralists of all history.[19] He wrote,

> Nature has determined woman's destiny through beauty, charm, and sweetness. Law and custom have much to give women that has been withheld from them, but the position of women will surely be what it is: in youth an adored darling and in mature years a loved wife.[20]

In early marriage, Freud tried to educate his wife according to his standards, but she just could not get excited about philosophy, science, and English. As he became more and more involved in his work, his interest in her waned. His intense schedule and the way he planned his vacations confirm his lack of involvement in family life. Freud may have drawn upon his own experience for his theorizing about the relations between the sexes. They were both cool and objective.

Freud discovered that sexuality does not begin in adulthood, but early in childhood. He did not mean simply that children have sexual feelings but that in childhood love is a problem. Love begins to be a problem in childhood and it continues to be a problem throughout life. Freud pictured childhood as invariably unhappy. This ancient and lasting pain is produced by something beyond all the problems our parents caused by lack of understanding. It is beyond the problems of being a lonely child. Freud was saying that something in the heart of love itself makes love pathetic.[21]

According to Freud, the sexual impulse always leads to dissatisfaction. Love begins in self-love (narcissism) which is self-deluding. Then, as love grows out of infancy into childhood, there are the inevitably frustrated incest impulses of the child and the competitions with siblings for parental love, and the inevitable enmity with those siblings. Finally, there is the disappointment lurking in all adult love. Freud felt that all love is blind. In love,

> the subject becomes, as it were, intellectually infatuated (that is, the powers of judgment are weakened) by the mental achievements and perfections of the sexual object and he submits to the latter's judgments with credulity.[22]

Freud calls sexuality "the most unruly of all the instincts." The reason that "the value the mind sets on erotic need instantly sinks as soon as satisfaction becomes readily attainable" is that later loves are only surrogates for the original one. The incest taboo frustrates the child's desires, but the instinct remains related to its first object. The force of these original passions explains for Freud the individual's restiveness within monogamy and also accounts for the fatigue of promiscuity. Far from being a champion of unbridled sensuality, Freud understood the close connection between the libertine and the ascetic. Both are excesses deriving from childhood's insatiable love of authority figures. If Jesus proclaimed the authority of love, Freud uncovered the love of authority. Both a St.

Augustine and a de Sade may be understood as fixated on the fantasies formed during childhood, "which have later, after all, found a way out into real life." Romantic love was similarly explained as "overvaluation." It rests on the delusion that the loved one is

> unique . . . irreplaceable, (and) can be seen to fall just as naturally into the context of the child's experience, for no one possesses more than one mother, and the relation to her is based on an event that is not open to doubt and cannot be repeated.

So we all live trapped in a series of erotic illusions.[23]

Freud saw his task as uncovering and describing these basic unconscious forces, which when known, could be controlled and harnessed for human betterment.

Understanding women was a puzzle Freud never solved. He asked a question he never answered, "What does Woman want?" He came closest to his answer with his idea that woman was an imperfect man, and hence his inferior. According to Freud, a woman during childhood believes herself to be a castrated male and spends the rest of her life trying to gain a symbolic penis. He suggested that her intellectual inferiority is undoubtedly due to the inhibition of thought caused by sexual repression. He noted that American women led men around by their noses which resulted in the "rule of women" in America. He was asked if he did not think it would be best if both partners in marriage were equal. Freud replied, "There must be inequality, and the superiority of the man is the lesser of the two evils."[24]

When he theorizes on love Freud reflects the prejudices of his day and his own inability to give of himself intimately and warmly without reservation. The notion that people can gain from loving others (in addition to satisfying specific instinctual needs) was as foreign to Freud as taking his wife on a vacation.[25]

And so we come to the end of this hurried view of our common sexual history. It has not been simple, but neither is the subject. Maybe it has helped to prepare us to accept a little more gracefully our present confusions and uncertainties.

2
Biblical Background

The Bible is a library of many books written over a period of one thousand years. It is about one thing, the relationship between God and human beings. It is in two parts because the Biblical belief is that there was an old relationship, or covenant, and a new relationship established by Jesus Christ. The Bible is our primary source for understanding these relationships. For that purpose it is authoritative. But it was not written to be authoritative about anything else. There are many other things in the Bible, but they are peripheral to the main purpose. When we go to the Bible to find out what it has to say about other things, such as sexuality, we must remember that it was not intended to speak as authoritatively on any other subject as it does on the two testaments. The Bible is not the word of God about everything.

In looking at the Bible for what it has to say about sex, we ought to understand first the cultural context, since what we find in the Old Testament was largely a reaction not only to sexual abuse within the community, but also to its abuse in the culture that surrounded it. The Fertility Cults were the main threat to Israel. They worshiped a mother-goddess who personified fertility. With her was a young male god who died and came to life again like the seasonal changes of vegetation. When he was absent from the mother-goddess, there was infertility in the earth, man, and beast. His consort mourned and searched for him. When he returned, fertility was renewed and restored and everyone rejoiced.

The fertility cults had a complete mythology of

sex. Worship involved sacral sexual intercourse by priests and priestesses and other specially consecrated persons. There were also sacred prostitutes of both sexes whose use was intended to emulate and stimulate the deities to bestow fertility. In these cults the barriers between the world of the gods and the world of man were very easily crossed. Thus, to have intercourse with a sacred prostitute was to enter into the world of the gods and to be involved in the mythological action that brings about order and fertility to land and people. Sex therefore was divinized. It was also ritualized into being the action through which the natural world and the spirit world became one.[1]

No doubt, many Israelites were tempted by the seductive lure of these rites and succumbed to them. They were practiced at numerous places all over the land. There was a sacrifice or common meal; wine was consumed in great quantity, which induced ecstatic frenzy which sometimes was climaxed by self-laceration and even self-emasculation. Child sacrifice was also practiced.

Against all this the prophets railed. It was totally against the ethical demands of Israel's god. Yahweh was the creator, which meant he was apart from his creation. He created sexuality, he was not embroiled in it. Consequently, sex was understood by Israel as a purely creaturely phenomenon. It was secular and, thus, subject to human control. Israel was unique because its god was transcendent and therefore beyond sexuality. To be sexual belongs only to creatures. Therefore, God is neither male nor female, although when Israel talked about God in anthropomorphic terms, it could only describe his transcendence as masculine, since it was masculinity that connoted power and authority. He is Father and Creator without the aid of a female counterpart.

Let us look at Genesis. The first creation story is the latest and most sophisticated. The second, beginning at 2:4b, is the oldest and most primitive. We will take them in the order we find them. In 1:27 we have an amazing statement about human sexuality. It was written probably in the fifth century B.C. by a group of priests while in Babylonian captivity. It says a lot:
1. Human beings were created in the image of their creator.
2. Males and females were created at the same time, equal.
3. The image of God in which they were created is to be found in maleness and femaleness (the original Hebrew says "penis and vagina created he them").

It is the third point that shocks us, and I must admit this is not the only way to interpret this verse, but let me make the case. God made humankind as a being-in-relationship. Persons were created to have a life which is one of relationship with God and with another like him/herself. This relational element in his being is the image of God in humankind. God, in his own being, is in fellowship. He is a Trinity. Since God is not a solitary being, so humankind in his image is also not alone. Humankind's humanity is essentially freedom in fellowship. And the fundamental form of this fellowship is that of being male and female. The image of God in humankind has always been a profound mystery, and so does human sexuality continue to be a profound mystery. They may be the same thing.

Genesis 2:18-23 is the more primitive story and was probably written in the tenth century B.C. But it was not very primitive for its time. Its pagan counterpart would have been the idea found in Plato's *Symposium* that Zeus split the original human being in two halves as a punishment for having tried to scale heaven. There sex is a punishment; here, in Genesis, sex is a creative act of God, originated because man's nature is such that it is not good that he should be alone. The context of God's creation of sexuality is the garden of Eden. The perfect place. Thus, sex is not the result of any problem; it is part of the perfection. It could also be said that in this story of creation the order of creation is from the lower to the higher. Woman's having been created last certainly does not imply any subordination. The idea of man's ruling over woman comes in this story after the Fall and is therefore thought of as the result of sin, not anything God had in mind originally.[2]

All through the Old Testament sexuality is an important part of life and was often seen as closely connected with other serious occasions. When oaths were made, the male sex organs were held. One absolutely serious part of life was linked with the seriousness of sexuality (Genesis 24:2-3, 9; Genesis 47:29). The rite of circumcision was not only the way one became a Jew but was obviously a dramatic way of saying that the covenant bond between God and man had an effect on a man's sexual style. Circumcision was something that was not "seen." The exposure of one's private parts was a strong taboo in Israel. Therefore, religion, with its sign, entered into the most intimate and secret part of the person.

The fact that nakedness was bad did not mean that for Jews the body was evil. The body was neither defamed nor deified. It was good because everything God created was good. Luther cleverly pointed out that the Lord, who was sinless, had a body and that the devil, who is sinful, is without a body.[3] The body is essential for being a person. After forming man "from the dust of the ground," God "breathed into his nostrils the breath of life. Thus the man became a living creature" (NEB). Consequently, we should not think of a person as an incarnated soul, but rather as an animated body. Our bodies are not encumbrances, they are essential to our being. That is why the distinctive Christian doctrine of the afterlife, based on our Jewish roots, is not one of immortality, but of resurrection, in which the body will be a perfect instrument of the spirit.[4]

After the Fall, the accounts of sexual love in the Old Testament often seem far from loving. The emphasis was usually on the procreative function. Monogamy was the usual but not exactly the ideal, since the more wealth a man had the more wives he accumulated. Polygamy and concubinage were condoned. Women were valued for their ability to bear children and not much else. And a woman had better feel insecure in her marriage if she did not produce a male child. The story of David and Michal (1 Samuel 18:20+) is a typical example. She is described as "loving" him, but nothing is similarly forthcoming from his side. David later took two other wives and numerous concubines. He was not faithful. He committed adultery with Bathsheba, had a child by her, and arranged to have her husband killed. Polygamy, adultery, incest, rape, and sexual perversion are all a part of the story of the chosen people. And yet there are moments of the deepest kind of human love. That between Jacob and Rachel started out as romantic as any on record. He had to work for fourteen years to get her, and their love lasted until Rachel's untimely death in childbirth.

The entire Song of Songs is a paean of praise to sexual love. It is so explicit that it is seldom read in public. (And interestingly enough, it is completely devoid of male arrogance.) The Old Testament knows all the shades of human love.

The story of the first testament is full of problems

between God and Israel. But again and again the image of marriage is used to describe what the relationship ought to be. The prophets often portrayed the fallenness of the covenanted people by the imagery of a woman unfaithful to her marriage vows. The threat of divorce is there until Hosea discovers that if he can love his wife when she is continually unfaithful to him, so must God love Israel even when Israel is "whoring after other gods." Out of the history of this struggle between God and his people, there emerged a consciousness of the strict connection between the good creation, the covenant, and the marital relation. In Judaism, the male-female relationship which once symbolized the ambivalence of the pagan world becomes the symbol of reciprocity of God's love for the people he has made his own, and their love for him. As this is seen to be the meaning of the holy, so is the marital relation changed into a religious sign of the covenant.

When we move from the Old Testament into the New Testament, we find a distinct difference in the way sexual relations are understood. Jesus is the source of all this. His statements are revolutionary. Deuteronomy (24:1-4) had permitted a husband to divorce his wife for "uncleanness." All he had to do was give her a certificate so that she might marry again.[5] In Jesus' time divorce had become a mockery. A contemporary rabbi propounded that a man might divorce his wife if she cooked his food too much! Another argued that he might properly divorce her if he sees a woman fairer than she![6] Jesus' attitude toward divorce is a shocking repudiation of the law and of the customs of the time. He said that Moses allowed divorce on account of the hardness of men's hearts, but God's intention was that marriage should be permanent. Jesus thus contradicted the law and yet did it on the basis of affirming and restoring a principle which had existed "from the beginning of creation" in the design of God (Mark 10:6). (Most modern critics regard Matthew's addition of "except on the ground of unchastity" as an addition to the original tradition.) Another instance of the difference between Jesus and the Old Testament is the penetrating practical implication of Christian love in Matthew 5:28, ". . . if a man looks on a woman with a lustful eye he has already committed adultery with her in his heart." To the Christian man every woman is a sister, respected as a person, who cannot be treated or even thought of as an object of his lust.[7] In the first example Jesus may be understood as reestablishing a law even more primitive than Deuteronomy, but in the second there is no doubt he has given the world something radically new: the new law of love. And this new law is much more basic than any of the old "laws." In fact, the "laws" are now seen to be what they truly are: guidelines toward loving. Therefore, Christians will always be cautious in making any law an absolute. The only absolute is the law of love. Even Jesus' new "law" against divorce must be ready to bow to the higher law of love. At times the most loving thing to do is to accept divorce.

Jesus did not display an ascetic attitude toward things sexual. One line in Matthew might seem to contradict this (19:12): ". . . there are eunuchs who have made themselves eunuchs for the sake of the kingdom of heaven." Jesus said this right after his statement about staying married, which seems to indicate that he meant some men who are married to unfaithful wives should be commended for patiently and chastely awaiting their return.[8] Some commentators in the past have seen this passage as a sympathetic reference to a radical form of sexual asceticism — castration. Origen, the great third century biblical scholar and spiritual writer, in an excess of ascetical zeal, mutilated himself after misinterpreting this passage by taking it in a literal sense. More likely, it was originally a recognition that the service of God may at times demand a self-imposed continence.

Another rigoristic saying is Luke 14:26: "If anyone comes to me and does not hate his father and mother and wife . . . he cannot be a disciple of mine." This seems to be a very anti-marriage statement. But it need not be interpreted in that fashion. In the first place, the word "wife" does not appear in the parallels in the other gospels.* Luke may have added this because of his "Ebionism."[9] Ebionites were a very early Jewish Christian sect which practiced extreme asceticism. But, in any case, the statement is not against marriage as such any more than it is opposed to any human relationships if they supplant in importance the commitment to Christ and the Kingdom. According to the Bible, marriage is part of God's creation and therefore good. Jesus would call it into question only if it becomes the center of one's ultimate concern. Then it takes on the role of an idol. The worst sin, according to the Bible, is idolatry, that is, putting something which is not God in the place of God. Jesus says in all three gospels that in the life after death there will be no marriage (Mark 12:25). But again this need not be understood as negative toward marriage. It could mean that marriage here on earth is a way of experiencing that intimate loving relationship with one other person which in the life hereafter we will be able to enjoy with everyone. With that interpretation this verse becomes the greatest compliment to marriage that has ever been made!

Jesus had comparatively little to say about the sins of the flesh. At times he seemed to regard them with a

---

*It does appear in Mark 10:29 KJV. But modern translations omit "wife" because it only appears in later manuscripts of Mark.

certain amount of tolerance. He did not consider them the worst of sins.[10] The incident of the woman taken in adultery (John 8:3-11) is a microcosm of Jesus' ethic. The textual history of this passage is unusual. It is omitted by all the chief manuscripts except one. In a secondary group of manuscripts, it appears at the end of John's Gospel, while in another it is placed after Luke 21:38. Many of these manuscripts mark it with an asterisk as doubtful, or place it in the margin, or add it on new leaves. Its vocabulary is not Johannine, and several words are characteristic of Lukan writings. All this does not necessarily mean that the passage is not authentic. It more probably is a strong indication of the problems the early Church had with the story. They must have feared that it would prove subversive of moral discipline. Jesus' opponents were not concerned to find out what his attitude was toward women. They were rather using her case to trap Jesus in a dilemma. They thought that either he had to uphold the Jewish law, and thereby get himself into trouble with the Roman authorities by illegally inciting others to kill the woman, or he must set aside the law and thereby be caught condoning a heinous sin. They certainly exposed their prejudice. They did not bring the man, too. Actually all the laws to which they were appealing demanded that both the man and the woman should be killed. Jesus' concern was not so much with the woman's act as with herself as a person who needed understanding and forgiveness. He was not shocked by her sexual sin. He did not delight in a self-righteous denunciation. Sensuality was in his eyes a minor vice beside the enormous spiritual pride of her accusers. He made them face this by asking the one without sin to cast the first stone. It is an amazing scene. Jesus did not condone her act, but he seems to have recognized that the sins of the flesh are not to be cured by fierce denunciation of them. Bad desires can be changed best by putting good ones in their place. So Jesus spent time with the morally disreputable to help them receive God's love and forgiveness and inspire them to want to be a part of the kingdom he was bringing. Let us not miss the by-product of his loving forgiveness of the woman: his devastating rebuke to male arrogance.

There is another event in the life of Jesus that seems to have some sexual overtones. It is the story of the woman who anointed Jesus' feet with ointment (Luke 7:36-50). She was called a sinner, which probably means she had been a prostitute. Tradition identifies her with Mary Magdalene. Her hair was down, which in the presence of men would seem highly immodest. She was crying tears of repentance or joy for what Jesus had meant to her. To wet his feet with her tears, to wipe them with her hair, and to kiss his feet, would all be seen as very personal, even intimate, activities. That a woman, especially of her sort, could feel such freedom in Jesus' presence must have offended and baffled those who saw it. Jesus might have been for her the first man who had ever treated her as a person rather than a sex object. Again it is the other man in the story who comes off badly. Simon thought he knew more about the woman than Jesus did. He therefore belittled Jesus for not acting according to his standards. The truth was, he knew less about the woman, and thus exposed in his own nature a hard, sophisticated arrogance. The astonishing thing in this story, though, is the relaxed, open acceptance by Jesus of a situation which, because of its sexual elements, would have upset and embarrassed almost any other man.

Jesus' attitude toward women and his relationship with them are among the amazing things reported in the New Testament. This is particularly striking when we realize how alien the environment around him must have been to such behavior. C. F. D. Moule says it very well:

> It is difficult enough for anyone, even a consummate master of imaginative writing, to create a picture of a deeply pure, good person moving about in an impure environment, without making him a prig or a prude or a sort of "plaster saint." How comes it that, through all the Gospel traditions without exception, there comes a remarkable firmly-drawn portrait of an attractive young man moving freely about among women of all sorts, including the decidedly disreputable, without a trace of sentimentality, unnaturalness, or prudery, and yet, at every point, maintaining a simple integrity of character?[11]

The social situation, as far as we can tell, seems to have been one of repressiveness and prudishness which went along with high moral standards, but which did not allow women much freedom, or men much companionship with women outside matrimony. Given that environment, no one could have invented the Gospel portrait of Jesus. It must have been that the absolutely unique personality of this man forced its way through an atmosphere completely opposed to it and totally uncomprehending. Moule goes on to say:

> ... the extraordinary thing is that writers who must themselves have hated and feared the very risks they are describing and who were themselves not wholly free from a repressive attitude, yet, despite themselves, succeed in presenting a strangely convincing picture of Jesus — a young, unmarried man — allowing himself to be fondled and kissed by such (disreputable) women, without either embarrassment or acquiescence in their morals. The simplicity and sure-footedness of the delineation are amazing. Jesus simply accepts these women as persons: compassionately and with complete purity and simplicity he accepts their affection while moving them to repentance.[12]

Very early in Jesus' ministry, Luke (8:1-3) mentions the fact that a group of women disciples accompanied him on his preaching mission along with the Twelve.

This was unprecedented. It was customary then for only young men to follow after a charistmatic leader. An anti-Christian author, Joachim Kahl, has interpreted all this quite differently. He claims that the New Testament defames sexuality.

> The defamation of sex inevitably leads to the defamation of women, who tend to be regarded as inferior beings. The New Testament provides plenty of evidence of this attitude. What is common to all its authors is a traditionally Jewish patriarchal view which was unable to concede equality of women. The gospels, for example, depicted Jesus as a man who treated women as second-class people, someone who certainly allowed himself to be served, looked after and supplied with money by them . . . but who did not accept any into the intimate circle of the twelve . . .[13]

But the position of the women who followed Jesus was no more demeaning than that of their leader. Luke uses the same verb "to wait on" to refer to what the women did for him and what he came to do himself: ". . . I am among you as one who serves" (Luke 22:27). Another interesting fact is that with all the caustic criticism that Jesus received, there is no instance recorded of women being hostile to him. Why were women so drawn to him? Dorothy Sayers, in her little pamphlet, *Are Women Human?* says,

> They had never known a man like this Man . . . who took their questions and arguments seriously; who never mapped out their sphere for them, never urged them to be feminine or jeered at them for being female.[14]

These women, some widows probably, and some presumably wives of the male disciples who followed Jesus throughout the length and breadth of Israel, remained faithful even to the end. While of the males, one betrayed him, another denied him, and most forsook him, a group of women were present at the crucifixion.

The most amazing single incident in the New Testament is the resurrection of Jesus from the dead. It is almost unbelievable that this greatest element of the Good News should have been first revealed to the world by the witness of a woman! A woman's witness was discounted as worthless in Israel. Josephus, the great Jewish historian, says, "Let not the testimony of women be admitted."[15] Could a greater thing have been done to begin the liberation of women than this?

Now let us try to deal with the most difficult subject of all: the sexuality of Jesus himself. Was Jesus married? The subject has never been seriously discussed until very recently, unless one wants to include such unorthodox theologians as Brigham Young, who had his own reasons for studying the case. He wrote:

> Jesus Christ was a practical polygamist; Mary and Martha, the sisters of Lazarus, were his plural wives, and Mary Magdalene was another. Also the bridal feast at Cana of Galilee, where Jesus turned the water into wine, was on the occasion of one of his own weddings.[16]

Just a few years ago, William E. Phipps wrote a book called *Was Jesus Married?* According to his research, the answer should be "probably." He feels that in the Palestine of his day, it would have been very unusual had Jesus not been married early in his life before his public ministry began. In view of the silence from the sources we have, Phipps concludes that it is unlikely that Jesus was married during his ministry. For the same reason, no data, he also thinks that from that probable early marriage, which ended before his ministry, there were no children. Phipps based his conclusions on what was the norm in New Testament times among Jews. They all got married. Life-long celibacy was completely foreign to that culture, and virginity was more of an embarrassment than a virtue. J. A. T. Robinson, in his book *The Human Face of God* (p. 56), says about this controversy:

> The decisive argument against Jesus' being married . . . is not the silence of the gospels . . . but 1 Corinthians 9:5 "Have I no right to take a Christian wife with me, like the rest of the apostles and the Lord's brothers, and Cephas?" If Jesus, like his brothers, had been known to have been married, it is inconceivable that Paul would not have appealed to the fact.

Phipps probably has not convinced many people, but he has made a significant point: Jesus was fully human and therefore partook of the sexuality that is a part of all of us. Jesus was not "above" sexual impulses or feelings. Not to have them is no longer thought of as better in any sense. We do not have any data to go on in this area; but faith would tend to find virtue in the way Jesus handled the same drives we are coping with, not in any deliverance from them. If Jesus is thought of as someone without sexuality — never even tempted by sex — then it would be hard to convince anyone that the Christian God looks favorably upon the sexual life of humanity. This would imply that the Christ redeems us *from* sexuality, it being the part of our nature he did *not* share. A sexless Jesus simply cannot be thought of as fully human. An heretical tendency in the early church which wanted to eliminate any humanity from the Christ was known as Docetism. If, as we believe, the Gospels do not want to present a Docetic Christ, why are they so silent in regard to Jesus' sexuality? Tom F. Driver wrote a perceptive article on this subject over fourteen years ago, in which he presents the best answer I have found to this question. He says that this silence may occur for a very positive reason.

> Few characteristics of the Gospels separate them more sharply

> from the literature of other savior figures and religious heroes
> than their abstention from representing their protaganist *either*
> as a champion of sexual renewal or as a warrior against the
> "demonic" sexual force. This is astonishing. Almost all
> religions make sexuality a principal concern. Either they regard
> it as a sign of power that must be replenished from on high, or
> they regard it as a pollution of which man must be purged.
> From the point of view of comparative religion, it is not
> surprising at all that Christianity as a religion brought forth
> monasticism, made a cult of virginity, and elevated its God-
> man above all sexual feeling. What is surprising is that the
> Gospels show in Jesus himself no sufficient basis for these
> attitudes . . . Over against the pagan gods and the pagan
> religions, we may say that Jesus appears as the great
> neutralizer of the religious meaning of sex. He does not, it is
> clear, regard sexuality as a mystical force emanating from the
> God-head. Jesus is no Dionysius. But contrary to what many
> Christians have assumed, the Jesus of the Gospels is not plainly
> "anti-Dionysian" either. That is, he does not, as far as we can
> tell, regard sexuality as a force emanating from Satan.[17]

Sex, then, is seen as a neutral fact of life, neither mystical nor demonic. It is one of the "goods" of creation that human beings can use for good or evil.

Perhaps Jesus did not express himself sexually in any way that would obviously become part of his story. But does one have to be sexually active to be sexually authentic? Does it make more sense to believe that it is the fully sexual person who can decide what his sexual role will be without feeling manipulated by that aspect of his physical nature to "prove" to himself or anyone else that he is "normal" or "virile"?[18] It is probably very helpful for all of us that the New Testament does not tell us the way in which Jesus expressed his sexuality. If it had, no doubt some church leaders would have made a doctrine out of it, that the way Jesus did it was obligatory for all Christians.[19] As it is, each of us is free in love to determine, with the Spirit's help, what his or her sexual life-style will be.

There is another person we must look at in our survey of the New Testament's attitude toward our subject: St. Paul. He may have that "St." in front of his name, but in shifting from Jesus to Paul, we move from an ideal to a person very much like ourselves. In fact, many of us may easily feel quite superior to Paul in matters sexual. Paul was a man of his time. Paul wrote about the sins of the flesh because he was dealing with Gentiles, amongst whom moral laxity was common. This was not the case with the Jews. Paul's early writings are also filled with the expectation of the imminent end of the world, which would explain some of his negativity toward sexuality with its obvious orientation to the future. But Paul does come close to an almost scornful attitude toward women. They are told strictly how to dress their heads when they pray in public (1 Corinthians 11:5), and that they are not to say a word (1 Corinthians 14:34).

> A woman must be a learner, listening quietly and with due submission. I do not permit a woman to be a teacher, nor must woman domineer over man; she should be quiet . . . it was not Adam who was deceived; it was the woman who . . . fell into sin (1 Timothy 2:11, 12, 13).

And 1 Corinthians 11:3: ". . . what I want you to understand is that Christ is the head of every man, man is the head of woman . . ." And there is the text that contemporary fundamentalists and anti-feminists use as the solution to so many present ills:

> . . . show the younger women how they should love their husbands and love their children, how they are to be sensible and chaste, and how to work in their homes, and be gentle and do as their husbands tell them, so that the message of God is never disgraced (Titus 2:4, 5).

His great anti-marriage chapter is 1 Corinthians 7. There he writes, "The time we live in will not last long. While it lasts married men should be as if they had no wives . . ." This kind of teaching had its effect even when the world did not come to an end. It was the beginning of the long history of sexual asceticism in Christianity. As the German Karl Kraus wrote: ". . . the Christian night time came on and man found it necessary to slink towards love on tiptoe [and] he began to be ashamed of what he did."[20] Yet at times we find in Paul amazing statements such as: "The wife cannot claim her body as her own; it is her husband's. Equally the husband cannot claim his body as his own; it is his wife's" (1 Corinthians 7:4). This is a remarkable attitude, completely out of keeping with the spirit of the first century. And again we have from Paul that Magna Carta of male/female relations, Galatians 3:28:

> All baptized in Christ, you have all clothed yourselves in Christ, and there are no more distinctions between Jew and Greek, slave and free, male and female, but all of you are one in Christ Jesus.

Salvation means human beings-in-fellowship. In Christ, Paul is saying, the basic divisions of race, class, and sex are done away; not differences which enrich fellowship, but divisions which lead to hostility and exploitation. These have no more place in the church.

In Ephesians 5:31, 32, Paul's genius comes through again as he gives us a new and higher understanding of marriage than had ever been known before and certainly has never since been superseded. In talking about the mysterious unity that can be created in marriage, he calls it "one flesh," and then says, "This mystery has many implications; but I am saying it applies to Christ and the church." Paul sees an analogy between the relationship of husband and wife on the one hand and Christ and the church on the other. This means that for Paul a husband or wife is given to us as the "deputy" of Christ himself. And therefore a spouse is to be loved with as entire and exclusive a loyalty as we have for Christ. In this way,

the unity known within marriage clearly points **beyond** itself, to the eternal reality of Christ's unity **with** us. If the oneness is the thing that is alike in both **relationships**, then the point is that this mysterious **uniting** of two different people in marriage is not **something** which arises out of the physical and **material** aspects of the relationship, but is a result of spiritual conditions.

It is too bad that when we reach the end of this New Testament survey, we cannot leave it on the high, clear note sounded by Jesus instead of the many sounds, both high and low, that come from St. Paul. But after Jesus, we are dealing with the world which had to struggle, and not always well, with applying the Good News to the ethical problems of life. The following chapters will try to bring that struggle up to date.

3
Contemporary Theories of Sexuality

Human sexuality is mysterious and probably always will be. Anything we have to cope with continually and yet feel we do not understand very well produces anxiety. One of the psychological laws is "structure binds anxiety." So we human beings never stop trying to understand, to make some sense out of, to impose meaning and order upon this part of life and thereby reduce the anxiety. There are many possible theories, or philosophies about sexuality that can be found in our contemporary culture. In this chapter we will look at a few of these.

Sex as Pleasure

This is a position which begins with a belief everyone holds: sexual activities can produce pleasure. But then it goes on to declare that sexual pleasure is the purpose, end, and meaning of sexuality. The *Playboy* philosophy is the most common unsophisticated source of this view. Albert Ellis, a psychiatrist, takes this position and has said it very bluntly: "Sex is fun."[1] It is recreation and is aimed at no end or goal other than its own spontaneous expression and enjoyment. A more carefully reasoned version of this belief is found in Masters and Johnson's latest book, *The Pleasure Bond*. In a dialogue beginning on page 27, a woman says, ". . . all we're talking about is enjoyment and pleasure. Is that all there is to sex?" Virginia Johnson replies,

> . . . I hope you aren't underestimating the significance of

pleasure — and by pleasure I don't mean fun. I mean the authentic, abiding satisfaction that makes us feel like complete human beings. We don't experience pleasure in *anything* we do if it fails to fulfill us in some fundamental way. So the question isn't whether there is something more important that lies beyond pleasure. The question, it seems to me, is: What important considerations *precede* pleasure?

Later in the book there is an answer. Commitment is an important consideration because it guarantees pleasure.

They [speaking about a young couple] are describing the circle of commitment. Being together gives them satisfactions, including sex, that reinforce their decision to live together as a couple; these satisfactions, which are highly valued, must be safeguarded. Each partner, *to protect his or her own happiness, tries to sustain the other partner's happiness* (italics mine) so that their relationship will flourish; and these reciprocal efforts intensify the satisfactions they find in living together — which further strengthen their wish to remain a couple. *They live according to the commitment of mutual concern, and pleasure is the bond between them* (italics theirs).[2]

Of course, there is some truth here. Actions must produce some sort of pleasure (reward), or we do not continue them, but the pleasure must be a by-product rather than the direct goal. Freud is famous for establishing the pleasure principle as identical with motivation. While Freud understood how important a motive pleasure was, his work was toward proving its futility. He is the architect of a great revolt against pleasure, not for it. According to Philip Rieff, Freud knew that suicide pleases the suicide; sadism pleases the sadist. The pleasure principle is a very subjective one.[3] Pleasure cannot be an end in itself. Prescott Lecky in his book, *Self-consistency*, said he believed that there is only one source of motivation, namely, the necessity to maintain the unity and integrity of the person, but that as a result of attaining unity, the person derives pleasure. For him, pleasure is only a by-product and not the actual goal of life.[4] Individuals spend their time searching for their own identity. They put an enormous amount of strength and emotional investment into this search. For it to be successful they have to experience communion with another person at a very deep level. This is what the pleasure view of sex makes no allowance for. It may be pleasurable for the moment, but after intercourse for pleasure, people feel less themselves, not more. Sex for pleasure, without the deepening of personal understanding, is a violation of the great human quest for reality, for truth about the self and others. Sexual pleasure, when it is not tied to tender affection for a person loved in body and soul, does not possess the secret of its renewal. The imagination is drained in trying to renew it. If pleasure is the goal, one is thrown back toward solitude by pleasure itself.

Sex as Religion

It is not difficult to let these two great passions of humankind, sex and religion, become confused with each other. Love is the key in both cases, and usually, if one key opens two different locks, you can expect them both to gain you entrance into the same house. The problem began all the way back in the Old Testament. Natural religion is the quest of the human to establish contact with the gods that are beyond him. As Peter Berger wrote in a *Christian Century* article:

> The cult of sacred sexuality provided this contact in a way that was both easy and pleasurable. The gods were as close as one's own genitalia; to establish contact with them, when all was said mythologically and all was done ritually, one only had to do what, after all, one wanted to do anyway.[5]

The Prophets were loud in their denunciations of

sacred sexuality. Not because the Jews were sexually repressive or puritanical. They tended to be very relaxed about such things. The prophets were not against sex, they were against sacred sex. They were almost saying: "Go ahead, have your sexual pleasure — but do not make a religion out of it!" Why not? Because it violated that basic Jewish understanding of both God and human beings. Sacred sex was based on the idea that God and Nature were one and the same. Judaism said no. God was the creator, and therefore stood over and against his creation. Therefore, there was no way a person could make contact with God by fusing the self with nature. The God of Israel was utterly transcendent. He was thought of as always confronting the world with his "otherness" and with judgments. He was never an immanent presence. His effect on people was not to bring other-worldly ecstacy, like the cults of sacred sexuality; rather, he directed people back into the world to get his will done in human affairs.

The modern world is not without its sacred sexuality cults. Some of the present revolt against Christian standards arises out of an assertion of the positive power of sexuality to express, communicate and release the self. The modern heresy is that sexual satisfaction constitutes the good life. Sex, for many, has become the way of salvation.[6] D. H. Lawrence was the great modern prophet of this faith.

> And God the Father, the Inscrutable, the Unknowable, we know in the flesh, in woman . . . In her we go back to the Father; but like the witnesses of the transfiguration, blind and unconscious.[7]

Norman Mailer is a more contemporary member of this cult. I think it was he who called woman ". . . a groined archway into the infinite."[8] The new sacred sexuality takes many different forms. It appears in various therapeutic cults: the "new sensitivity," the occult, some oriental sects. As in all heresies, the problem is in an over-emphasis on something good until it loses its proper place in a balance with other goods. Dorothea Krook is a thinker who, from the Christian perspective, may have the clue to restoring the balance. She says:

> Is it not the mystery of the Incarnation that most fully and most powerfully illuminates, espresses, indeed *defines,* the mysterious and wonderful communion of spirit achieved by a husband and wife in the bodily consummation of their love; and is not therefore the act of sexual union in the profoundest sense a "figure" of the incarnation — the Word, which is love, made flesh? . . . It is the man and the woman to whom the act remains, each time, as fresh and beautiful as it was the first time, who are able to sustain and perpetuate their first sense of its glory in the midst of the sober or bleak or sordid realities of day to day life, and who can feel, afresh each time, a boundless gratitude for each other and for this blessed source of sweetness and strength — it is they who are truly "virgin," the truly pure and chaste; and . . . it is they who are the remnant selected by grace to be the true and spiritual seed of the risen Christ.[9]

That is as near to Christianizing sacred sexuality as I can imagine. It is certainly a New Testament theme that is sounded by Miss Krook: the love of man and woman is an image of the love of God for humankind. But there is one point that ought to be added. Sexual love must know its limitations. The unconscious, the libido, the Id, from which much of it arises, are a complex set of forces, not all of which are loving. There are also fear, hate, self-preservation, and their opposite, the death wish. Therefore, we must be aware of human limitations and frustrations, and even evils in this, as in all aspects of human nature. And certainly the discovery of the meaning of love is not limited to one kind of fulfilling experience. Sexual fulfillment is only one way. The heresy comes in when we make sex "all important." This is idolatry. The truth is that the most satisfying experience of sensuality comes when it is not made into a religion — when it is not in the center of things — but has its rightful and limited place as one among many aspects of being human.

Sex and Idealism

By this title I mean the belief (by some considered ultra-liberal) that there is a significant continuity between our highest sexual aims, insights and aspirations on the one hand and the nature of ultimate reality on the other. So let us probe into the question: What is the human sex drive? For a long time the answer to this question was put into a mechanistic-hydraulic model. By this model, instinctual energy is always being created inside the person, and contained by damming up, and controlled by "sluice gates." Freud advanced this theory that the libido expands, tensions increase, and discomfort rises until some action (such as orgasm for the sexual instincts) releases the tension pleasurably, and the cycle is ready to start all over again. This mechanical model of the body has given rise to the popular interpretation of feelings and emotions which sees them as something we do not consciously intend. They are a non-rational push from inside ourselves that drives toward satisfaction and relaxation, but not toward any meaning. We simply have an inner secretion of adrenalin or gonadal production, and the resulting need to let off our anger or sexual excitement. Some object that can be the target for this drive must be found. As Rollo May says in his book, *Love and Will*, it is a very common assumption in our day that feeling is a subjective push from inside you.

Emotions are forces which you put into motion, and so are to

> be "emoted" in whatever way you happen to feel at the moment... What is omitted [in this] view is that emotions are not just a push from the rear but a pointing toward something, an impetus for forming something, a call to mold the situation.[10]

Feelings, therefore, are not just a chance state of the moment, they are *intentional*. Erich Fromm believes that in humankind there emerges character as distinct from instincts. These emotions are rooted in this character and not simply in psychological needs. He illustrates this by saying that a man may prefer to think of himself as being simply oversexed. He uses the old theory to convince himself that he has an overgenerous supply of instinctual drive. But if one thinks of the source of his actions not in sexual instincts, which man does not have, but in character, then we begin to explain things differently. It may be that he is simply over-vain.[11] What that man wants to think of as sexual drive can be understood better as coming from his character: he is bored, or he has a wish for power over people, or he is lonely, or anxious, or it may even be that he wants to express love. Humankind's biological processes and sexual organs are not separated from, but integrated into, the whole human personality. A human is the peculiar creature who lives both a biological and psychic existence at the same time. While sexual activity is common to both humans and animals, what is communicated through human sexual behavior is never understood by looking at the biological element only. For humans, the organic urges and acts are never detached from the search for personhood. That search may be successful or destructive, wholesome or corrupted, but it is always the self's search for belonging through communication with another. The facts of life are always intimately bound up with the meaning of life.

Human beings are aware of the fact of their

sexuality, but they do not have any intuitive understanding of its significance. This is beautifully symbolized in the Genesis myth when Eve is created out of Adam's rib. During all this, Adam is unconscious. He does not know what is going on, and the divine secret of what God was up to has never been fully revealed. Sex remains a profound and baffling enigma of personal life. Any answers that can be found will arise out of the right kind of encounter between the sexes. Here again the Genesis myth is suggestive. God brings Adam and Eve together. God provides the context for this meeting, and in it, they each perceive in the other a likeness to the self, and a difference. In the permanent commitment to each other, they become aware of a new unity-in-diversity that is so intense they call it "one-flesh." The meaning of sexuality, then, is to be discovered, not in probing the complexities of the individual, although that must be the prerequisite, but through an experience of responsible personal relationship with the sexual "other." As in all other aspects of human life, humans exist in relationship, in dialogue with another. Understanding, then, comes from the proper kind of relating which enables one to sympathetically stand where the other is standing.[12] True sexual knowledge, then, is always existential. One writer on this subject, Derrick Bailey, thinks that this kind of knowledge is not the kind that can be expressed or communicated in any way. Rather, it is an interior awareness of the meaning of manhood or womanhood which is experienced only in the immediacy of sexual encounter, and disappears with the termination of meeting. He goes on to say,

> Reflection upon past encounters may bring consciousness of having once known, and the anticipation of knowing again, but the content of the knowledge itself can neither be recalled nor predicted. Nor can such knowledge ever be other than

> fragmentary, particular, and impossible to generalize or formulate; the full meaning of sex always remains God's secret, and all human insight here is at best but clouded and imperfect. In so far as Man attains any degree of understanding it is due to the quality of his sexual relationships — and right relationship, therefore, is ultimately the only source of sound sexual values and a true conception of sex.[13]

In 1974 Ernest Becker got a Pulitzer Prize for his book, *The Denial of Death*. His main point was that people's innate fear of death is the true driving force behind all their activities. In this view everything people do can best be understood as an attempt to transcend the inevitable, death. Becker thinks that sexuality is one of the major ways human beings try to avoid their creatureliness, particularly in contemporary society where for many people religion has been discarded. According to Becker, religion was at one time the major way people defeated death, but now religion has been replaced by sex. If you do not have a God in heaven, an invisible dimension that justifies the visible one, then you take what is nearest at hand: you grab onto a partner. One needs "somebody" with whom to grope for the meaning of one's life. And for a while this method gives real benefits.

> Is one oppressed by the burdens of his life? Then he can lay it at his divine partner's feet. Is selfconsciousness too painful, the sense of being a separate individual, trying to make some kind of meaning out of who one is . . . The one can wipe it away in the emotional yielding to the partner, forget oneself in the delirium of sex, and still be marvelously quickened in the experience. Is one weighted down by the guilt of his body, the drag of his animality that haunts his victory over decay and death? But this is just what the comfortable sex relationship is for: in sex the body and the consciousness of it are no longer separated; the body is no longer something we look at as alien to ourselves . . . Everything is "natural" . . . But we also know from experience that things don't work so smoothly or unambiguously . . . Sex is of the body and the body is of death.[14]

Becker explains this two ways. First, animals who procreate die. Their relatively short life span is somehow connected with their procreation. Nature conquers death not by creating eternal organisms but by having short-lived ones reproduce sexually. From the biological standpoint, this evolutionary process made it possible for really complex organisms to emerge instead of the simple — and almost literally eternal — self-dividing ones. But for humans, sex reminds us that we are simply a link in the chain of being. That is exactly what every human being does *not* want to be. He/she wants to be unique, with special gifts for the universe. Sex always has within it this double negative message: physical death and common species animality. From the very beginning man has

> brought sexual taboos into being because he needed to triumph over the body, and he sacrificed the pleasures of the body to the highest pleasure of all; self-perpetuation as a spiritual being through all eternity.[15]

Consequently, sex is a disappointing answer to the riddle of life. The sexual partner does not and cannot represent a complete and lasting solution to the human dilemma. If you find the ideal love and try to make that relationship the sole judge of good and bad in yourself, you lose yourself in the other, and that is idolatry again. What is it we want when we elevate the loved one to the status of God?

> We want redemption — nothing less. We want to be rid of our faults, of our feeling of nothingness. We want to be justified, to know that our creation has not been in vain . . . we expect them to "make us good" through love. Needless to say, human partners can't do this . . . Redemption can only come from outside the individual.[16]

Sex as Hot or Cool

For some of those who have gotten the word that sex cannot bring salvation, expectations have been lowered, and sex has become "cool." For those who still expect great things from it, sex is "hot." According to Anna K. and Robert T. Francoeur, the authors of *Hot and Cool Sex,* our culture is experiencing great tension over these two basic approaches. The essence of our Hot Sex culture is intercourse. The background is patriarchal. The male must be the active partner, dominating by brute strength and rational logic the female, whose virtues are those of passivity, obedience and dependence. Virginity may not last long in a Hot Sex culture, but it is an important symbol, in the Old Testament sense of preserving the saleability of the female as property. Of course this does not apply to the male, for whom virginity is frowned upon. As the King of Siam said to Anna in *The King and I,* "A girl must be like a blossom, with honey for just one man. A man must live like a honeybee, and gather all he can." For the Hot Sex male, any playmate will do. Personal physical pleasure is the prime concern; sensitiveness and responsibility are minor. One can escape the burdens of time, and aging, by multiplying experiences. The goal is possessing and conquering without investing any more of the self than is absolutely necessary. There is pressure to perform; on the male to prove himself every chance he gets, for the female to satisfy the male ego with mutual and/or multiple orgasms. With its ("Hot Sex") dualistic roots in the separation of soul and body, spirit and matter, male and female, it is hard for a Hot Sex male to accept the female as a person. The foregoing description does not leave much to value in the Hot Sex culture, and yet some genuine values may appear if we change the label from Hot Sex to

Passionate Sex. That sounds better, does it not? Now we can describe with less revulsion the burning desire, the gnawing tension, the almost savage hunger that human sexuality can produce. For many people sex would not be satisfying without the kind of emotional discharge that the passionate approach provides. It emphasizes the *yearning* for the person one is with, a *craving* to penetrate her and to be penetrated by him, a *striving* for the deepest contact, a *need* for emotional union, to appropriate the other, and possibly to give oneself as well. For most of us, the reference point for all this is probably what we remember from that youthful turmoil which everyone cherishes but no one manages properly when it first appears. Theodore Reik, one of Freud's disciples, has said that passionate love arises as part of the adolescent's attempt to fulfill some ego ideal. Having been frustrated in our striving for self-perfection, we transfer the image of this ideal to another person. Romantic love develops its ferocity from the desperate effort to rescue a menaced ego through the attempt to appropriate that perfect goodness promised by ego's illusory image of the beloved. And yet, passionate desire is not greater in those who are more dissatisfied with themselves. We all have the need for oneness with the other person which we achieve by means of our passion.

Cool Sex is the new approach. It may be new to twentieth century America, but, according to Irving Singer, the battle between the hot and cool approach has been going on in the Western world for 2,000 years.[17] Its basic thrust is the desire to have male-female relationships equal in every way, without sex stereotypes and fixed roles. It also wants to eroticize all of life, rather than making sex center primarily on intercourse. In Cool Sex culture, men no longer measure their identity as males in terms of aggressiveness, number of females conquered, or male progeny sired. And women can no longer find automatic social acceptability in the magical phrases, "his wife" or "their mother." Now male and female identities must come from within, from self-actualization.[18] Marriage and the male-female relationship take on a diffused, low-definition character. There is also an aspect of Cool Sex that emphasizes objectivity, detachment, and almost non-involvement. Anything goes in a Cool Sex culture, and this means not only tolerance, but the real possibility of alternate life styles for yourself as well as for others. The only basic rule is not to exploit others, sexually or otherwise. There is a single moral standard applying to both men and women, married or single. Sexual intercourse is seen as freed from the restrictions of procreation and therefore is a way of relating and knowing. Persons are unique, incomparable, valuable, and irreplaceable. So competition and jealousy are automatically eliminated. Human growth is a prime value in the Cool Sex culture, and growth is seen as happening mainly in interpersonal relationships. These should be involving and intimate. The belief is that no single relationship, no matter how intimate, can possibly fulfill all the needs of any one person. So the new ideal is for each person to develop several simultaneously close relationships that reinforce one another. In Cool Sex culture, the vast majority of one-to-one sexual relationships will begin with the normal period of romantic possessive exclusivity. But when they have satisfied this need, most will be forced to make a choice: to continue the closed union and risk disillusionment when its unrealistic Hot Sex expectations are not met, or to face the tensions and pain of opening up their marriage and creating a larger support system with new relationships and intimacies.

Again, the foregoing description might not appeal to a lot of you readers. Let us change the label again and see if it makes a difference. Let us call it not Cool Sex but Sensuous Sex. Sensuous Sex extols an easier, more delightful way of satisfying our sexual needs. Sensuous ways are based on a free aquaintance with the body rather than an emphasis on its emotional importance.[19] Sensuous Sex sees all sexual pleasure as simply enjoyable in itself. It does not necessarily lead on to anything else. An ordinary illustration of this is the male's pleasure in simply watching a female. It would be a pity to live with nothing but the sexual pleasure of looking. But one does not have to justify such interests by citing another activity to which they lead. The sensuous attitude is basically innocent. It is often a playful enjoyment of the body and of the human personality as it expresses itself through the senses. It can almost be called an aesthetic interest whose materials are sensations related to sexual pleasure. Whether its pleasures lead to orgasm or not, whether it limits itself to foreplay or goes beyond, whether with a single partner or many at once, whether heterosexual or homosexual, it can be approached as an artistic activity designed to maximize and prolong human pleasure.

> Stendhal gives the sensuous at least as much importance as the passionate: "To love is to derive pleasure from seeing, touching, and feeling through all one's senses and as closely as possible, a lovable person who loves us."[20]

I have not given you an exhaustive description of what their practitioners describe as Hot or Passionate Sex over against Cool or Sensuous Sex, but enough to get a feel for the conflict between the two, and maybe to help you begin to decide where you are yourself; hot, cool, or medium.

Sex and Theology

Christians believe that God took on human flesh in Jesus the Christ. This has a radical meaning for all of life: Flesh (a human being) and Spirit (God) were one in him. To believe this is to struggle against anything which would attempt to separate them. The most fleshly part of human life is sexuality. Christians will expect the Spirit to manifest himself most powerfully in this area. The Incarnation also tells us that God is not simply the ultimate everything of the philosophers. He is for us. He came to be with us. God is not just a "Being." He is a "Being-for." When St. Paul talks about all the things that can not separate us from the love of Christ (Romans 8:35f), he means nothing can, because of the nature of God. The "Being-for-ness" of God cannot be thwarted. If we believe that human beings are created in God's image, then we too are beings-for-others.[21] We come into the world incomplete. We long for the completion which comes from loving. We are designed "for-another." The sexual organs themselves are external signs of what we mean. They have no meaning in themselves, they point to the need for completion. So, the whole human personality is made to be fulfilled by loving and being loved by others. Sexuality then is a sign of the very law of our being, which is being-for-another.[22] "To be a person is to be essentially in search of a person."[23] The complementarity of male-female sexuality is the structure in the flesh that enables us to be-for-another and thereby know the Spirit in the flesh. The theological doctrine of original sin also has its application here. It is best stated as original righteousness, because the belief is that righteousness is more "original," more basic, than the sin which came later. But its common meaning now is that human beings have an innate capacity to foul up themselves. There is a basic egotism in each of us which makes us tend to give absolute significance to ourselves and to deny such a status to others. Sexual love is one of the greatest forces against this. In it, we know the absolute importance of another. And in knowing that, we realize our own absolute significance, which consists in our capacity to live, not only in ourselves, but in and for another.

Sexuality and religion both find satisfaction in losing the self in something greater. As Martin D'Arcy says, "We aspire to be loved by one whose love breaks down the last reserve of the self, so that we can belong utterly to him."[24] That idea can apply just as easily to our relationship with God or another human.

Reinhold Niebuhr clearly stated how easily sin enters human life in the sexual realm:

> The instincts of sex are particularly effective tools for both the assertion of the self and the flight from self . . . It is both a vehicle for the primal sin of self-deification and the expression of an uneasy conscience, seeking to escape from self by the deification of another.[25]

Let us look at one sexual sin more closely, that of lust. Jean-Paul Sartre in his book, *The Emotions,* claims that emotions are an attempt to change the world from what it really is to what we would like to have it. It is like magical thinking in the attempt to make the world suit us better by altering our reaction to the world. The emotion of lust, by this definition, could be understood as the imaginative changing of our actual relation to a person of the opposite sex, in favor of a different relationship which would give us more and different sexual satisfactions. Lust is magical thinking applied to sexual relationships. John Macmurray in his book, *Reason and Emotion,* claims that chastity is really nothing but emotional honesty. It is the ability to be truthful with feelings. We might combine these two ideas and say that chastity is facing the facts about our sexual relationships and not letting our imaginations, by magical thinking, construct a world that does not exist. Lust could then be seen as simply not being honest with the facts. The truth is not usually such as will support the actions which lust imagines, and therefore, if one is "true" to reality, or honest, or chaste, or realistic, one would not lust. Whereas, if the facts of a realtionship truly support the consummation of sexual union, in that case it would seem that lust is right and even appropriate. Lust is wrong when it is not "right," not true, not chaste, not a part of the facts of a sexual relationship.

The doctrine of the Trinity has an application to human sexuality, according to the great Russian lay theologian, Nicolas Berdyaev. In his book, *Freedom and the Spirit,* he says that Christianity solves the great problem of dualism; flesh vs. spirit, or God vs. man, in the God-man, Jesus. Duality is overcome by unity. But even a greater synthesis occurred when man was able to understand that the Son is God, the Father is God and also the Spirit is God. The Father loves the Son, the Son loves the Father, and the love between them is the Holy Spirit. Berdyaev goes on to apply this to human love. He says, "The meeting of one person with another always finds its fulfillment in a third . . . The life of man and of the world is an interior moment of the mystery of the Trinity."[26] He is saying that the Holy Spirit is the source of all love. When two people love each other greatly and know that there has arisen between them a new creation which they refer to as "our love," it is God the Holy Spirit who is involved. We love each other "in God" (as well as the more common expression, we love God in each other). Maybe we need to be less theoretical and more concrete about these ideas. Can anything be loved in anything else? Is this possible? Certainly. We often love ourselves in other people, like the parent who loves his own image in his child. We can love someone because he/she reminds us of someone else, like a parent, for instance. We can love something in a person which has not yet come out. This is future love. We can love that reality in another which is striving to exceed its own limits. In other words, we can love in someone else something greater than he/she is. As Ralph Harper has written:

> This is what it means to say we love God in someone else and, similarly, in our mutual love for each other. This is why lovers experience a sense of mystery beyond their understanding, not only in the gift to each other of love, but in the reaching out of love itself.[27]

But we also love others in God. Harper says,

> The force of the preposition "in" confirms the impression that lovers sometimes have that their love is not wholly their own but resides within a love greater than what they know each other to be capable of.[28]

Another Russian, Vladimir Solovyev, tries to throw light on the same mystery:

> Love . . . consists in the acknowledgment for another creature of unconditional significance . . . But we can assert . . . [this] only by faith, which is the assurance of things hoped for, the conviction of things not seen . . . we must, by faith in the object of our love, understand the affirmation of this person as he exists in God, and as in this sense possessing everlasting significance.[29]

Through all this Christians begin to understand how their own marriages can be something like "the spiritual marriage and unity betwixt Christ and His Church" — from the 1928 Prayer Book Marriage Service. Believing in that divine marriage, they feel liberated for their human marriages, and for the same close, mystical union with each other.

4
Male-Female Differences

One of the wisest of people, philosopher John Macmurray, has said that he thinks the problem of relations between men and women is the most important our age faces. And it is new. It is no longer the age-old battle between the sexes. We now face an entirely different problem. He explains:

> The development of civilization depends on the interplay of two factors, individual initiative and social cohesion. If the forces which maintain social cohesion manage to overcome individual initiative, civilization stagnates and deteriorates. If the forces making for . . . individualism . . . become overmastering, they disrupt social unity and produce a catastrophe. Roughly speaking, the intellect is on the side of individualism, while emotion is on the side of unity . . . when civilization began to develop, it was through the rise of individuals standing out from the mass who showed the capacity to act and think for themselves and so to become spear-heads of initiative . . . [That role] has been until recently almost completely confined to men. We might say with very great truth that when men took to being individuals — in thinking and fighting, and inventing, and creating — women took charge of the maintenance of social unity. So the sexes were differentiated in their social functions — man towards individuality and intellect, woman towards unity and emotion . . . In our own day, however, [this pattern] has been challenged with increasing success, not in theory but practically. Women have increasingly insisted that they too are individuals, and must be permitted to stand upon their own achievement; to realize their own capacities as individuals; to exercise their own initiative in the development of civilization . . . We cannot do other than look upon it as a momentous advance in culture and civilization . . . But it means in principle the disappearance of a differentiation of function which has governed the relation of the sexes from the dawn of history. No longer can we look to women to guard the delicate spiritual attitudes which maintain the unity of persons in the face of the differentiating forces of individualism — of private self-realization. No longer can men

specialize in the intellectual life while women specialize in the emotional. The social unity . . . must be maintained, if we are not to perish, but it can no longer be maintained through the differentiation of the social functions of the sexes . . . That is the crisis we are facing . . . [It] is a new one in a history of civilization . . .[1]

What Are the Specifics of the Problem?

Let us look first at what women are saying. They are objecting to: inequities in wages, sex discrimination in hiring, sexual harassment on the job, inequities in laws affecting marriage, the merchandising of sex appeal, sexist training of young children, the sexist structure of the English language, conservative abortion laws, the lack of child care facilities for working mothers, the brainwashing of girls into the wife, mother, homemaker roles, all power structures dominated by men, and marriage itself, to mention only a few.

If you asked foreigners to comment on American women they would most likely say, "They are pampered, spoiled, assertive, and independent." They think of America as a woman's paradise. And yet it is appropriate that there is a revolt in this paradise. With our country's ideals of independence and equality, its women are naturally going to be more conscious of inequities. If it is true that only a minority of America's women are disturbed, it is significant that the minority is at the top of the social scale: the wealthy and well educated. And when that group is dissatisfied, then tomorrow the masses will be too.

Freedom from male domination is the central thrust of the Women's Liberation Movement. But where is male domination most keenly felt? Some women answer, "in society"; others answer, "in bed." These two answers have produced the two great divisions in the movement. The first is interested in redressing wrongs suffered by women in employment and politics. The second believes that women are also subjugated in their roles as wives and mothers. The next big question is this: Is one of these problem areas the primary one that causes the second? "Yes," says one group, "The sexual domination of women is the source of all other oppression." They claim that "[women] . . . have been oppressed and degraded by a masculine culture that has treated them primarily as sexual objects, limited to pleasure and progeny."[2] These women we call the "environmentalists," because they feel that, since culture has created this terrible situation, culture can be changed. Basic to this hope is the belief that the essential differences between men and women are slight compared to those imposed by society. They also cite the enormous variations found between members of the same sex. So, they argue, the cultural pattern dictating the way the sexes relate *can* be changed.

But the environmentalists are opposed by those who do not think that women's problems in the state house and legislative chambers come ultimately from women's problems in the bedroom. These women are interested in the liberation movement, but they do not feel that the basic sexual relationship with men is the main problem. They feel that that area may require adjustments, but they are strongly opposed to any basic change in this part of a woman's life. These women we call the "eternal feminists." They believe that women and men are basically very different indeed. And there is nothing that anyone can do about these built-in, innate, unchangeable, and extremely important differences.

Freud started this line of reasoning when he said that anatomy is a woman's destiny. The importance of woman's procreative role is central in this argument. Childbirth is seen as the highest physical and emotional fulfillment for any woman, and the psychological and emotional traits that accompany motherhood are seen as the essence of psychic femininity.

Erich Fromm, in his *Art of Loving,* says the feminine character has the qualitities of productive receptiveness, protection, realism, endurance, motherliness.[3] Femininity, by this definition, is woman's most precious commodity. It is viewed as the equal of any masculine intellectual achievement. And this comes from nature, not culture. Therefore, trying to change this basic feminine difference, which is "given," is not only dangerous but ultimately impossible. So we see in these various views the fact that the Movement is far from being united either in deciding just what the most important problem is, or in determining the best route toward solutions.

Psychiatrist Ruth T. Barnhouse sees the background of the Women's Movement this way:

> Paradoxically, things were easier in a former age, which at least believed that women had special qualities and virtues, and which felt that they should be valued just because they were women. In our time, with women no longer on a pedestal or . . . in need of special protection, they are simply seen as competitors in a tight job market, and their devaluation and oppression takes place in cynical and subtle ways. This is reinforced by the excessively materialistic values of a rampantly commercial culture in which, in order to maximize the payoff to the exploiters, it is necessary to have a significant segment of society whose principal task is to be consumers. After the Second World War, middle-class women were the natural choice to fill this role, which very soon began to create in them the first symptoms of the psychological malaise that eventually erupted in the Women's Liberation Movement.[4]

A rather old style complaint or plea from a troubled "woman" appeared in a Roman Catholic paper in 1970. It almost sounds quaint now, but it does typify one approach to the problem:

> I am woman. I am your wife, your sweetheart, your mother, your daughter, your sister... your friend. I need your help. I was created to give the world gentleness, understanding, serenity, beauty, and love. I am finding it increasingly difficult to fulfill my purpose. Many people in advertising, motion pictures, television, and radio have ignored my inner qualities and have repeatedly used me only as a symbol of sex. This humiliates me; it destroys my dignity; it prevents me from being what you want me to be: beauty, inspiration, and love — Love for my children, love for my husband, love of my God and country. I need your help to restore me to my true position ... and allow me to fulfill the purpose for which I was created. I know that you will find a way.[5]

Most current statements by women could better be classed in the "verbal karate" category. (The phrase "verbal karate" reflects three things: 1. the fact that, as in actual karate, the momentum of one's opponent is used to win points; 2. the fact that women have felt themselves forced to take strong measures simply to get attention; and 3. the fact that males often find themselves reacting defensively and with bewilderment.) The following examples are from Robin Morgan's book, *Sisterhood is Powerful.*[6]

The average housewife works a 99.6 hour workweek — Chase Manhattan Bank.

Women are never able to have their own names. The "maiden name" belongs to your father; the "married name" belongs to your husband.

In ten out of fourteen clerical and office jobs, men got higher pay than women — for identical work — Equal Employment Opportunities Commission.

If I were asked ... to what the singular prosperity and growing strength of that people ought to be attributed, I should reply: to the superiority of their women — Alexis de Tocqueville *(Democracy in America,* 1840).

Women have served all these centuries as looking glasses possessing the power of reflecting the figure of man at twice its natural size — Virginia Woolf.

What we owe men is some freedom from their part in a murderous game in which they kick each other to death with one foot, bracing themselves on our various comfortable places with the other — Grace Paley.

Woman is the nigger of the world — Yoko Ono.

The Various Women's Organizations

In the fall of 1966 a small group of women gathered in Washington to found the National Organization for Women. It viewed itself as a kind of NAACP for women. It wanted to use partnership with men to gain economic, legal, and political rights for women. A typical statement from them on marriage is: "Marriage should be an equal partnership with shared economic and household responsibilities and shared care of the children..."[7]

A radical feminist group, "The Feminists," in New York shows clearly the difference between this kind of organization and the more conservative NOW. The former's policy statement on marriage is:

> Because the Feminists consider the institution of marriage inherently inequitable, both in its formal (legal) and informal (social) aspects, and because we consider this institution a primary formalization of the persecution of women, and because we consider the rejection of this institution both in theory and in practice a primary mark of the radical feminist, we have a membership quota: that no more than one-third of our membership can be participants in ... marriage. August 8, 1969.[8]

An example of an even more militant group is SCUM (Society for Cutting Up Men). Its Manifesto reads:

> Life in this society being, at best, an utter bore and no aspect of society being at all relevant to women, there remains to civic-

> minded, responsible, thrill-seeking females only to overthrow the government, eliminate the money system, institute complete automation, and destroy the male sex ... if a large majority of women were SCUM they could acquire complete control of this country within a few weeks simply by withdrawing from the labor force, thereby paralyzing the entire nation. Additional measures, any one of which would be sufficient to completely disrupt the economy and everything else, would be for women to declare themselves off the money system, stop buying, just loot, and simply refuse to obey all laws they don't care to obey. The police force, National Guard, Army, Navy, and Marines combined couldn't squelch a rebellion of over half the population, particularly when it's made up of people they are utterly helpless without ... [9]

WITCH (Women's International Terrorist Conspiracy from Hell) was born on Halloween, 1968, in New York and claims to promote a

> ... total concept of revolutionary female identity ... WITCH lives and laughs in every woman. She is the free part of each of us, beneath the shy smiles, the acquiesance to absurd male domination, the make-up or flesh-suffocating clothing our sick society demands ... If you are a woman and dare to look within yourself, you are a WITCH. You make your own rules. You are free and beautiful ... Whatever is repressive, solely male-oriented, greedy, puritanical, authoritarian — those are your targets ... You are a Witch by being female, untamed, angry, joyous, and immortal ... [Furthermore] Marriage is a dehumanizing institution — legal whoredom for women.[10]

How Are Men Reacting?

It seems as if all of this feminist revolution has come as a great surprise to most men. If it is true that they are the oppressors, then this is to be expected. The oppressors are never "ready" for a revolution that has designs on their power, and they also are not expected to "understand" it. So we have a good number of males who are opposed to any change in the male-female relationship, although they keep a low profile and are certainly not organized. But I would guess that by far the majority of American males have "gone along with" many aspects of the Women's Movement. During the Second World War, the well known G.I. definition of an ideal girlfriend was: "a beautiful, blond, deaf and dumb nymphomaniac who has no relatives and owns a liquor store." One cannot quite imagine that sort of definition being the current one today (even if we were in a war); maybe privately among a certain class, but not as a popular bit of male humor. Men in general have matured in this area. At least they are not as overtly male chauvinistic as they obviously were just a few years ago. The old sterotype of the he-man is fading fast. Long before John Wayne died, his image was culturally over the hill. Sure, we still have the Marlboro man, and new James Bond movies, and the *Playboy* male image has not changed much, but generally speaking most males have mellowed. And we have found out a few things too:

Richard the Lion-Hearted, the Crusader, troubadour; Achilles, who vanquished Hector before the walls of Troy; the fighting Spartans; the hard-riding Arab Sheiks; the ruthless Nazi Elite Corps — were all (or a high proportion of them) homosexuals. Everything has become more complicated, and masculinity along with it. So we are more tolerant and accepting of a much broader view of so-called "masculine" traits. And because of this new tolerance we have widened "femininity" to include much more freedom for women also.

Do Men Have Problems Too?

Yes, big ones. In fact one of the goals within the Women's Movement is to liberate men from the old rigid understanding of what a "man" is supposed to be. Sexism cuts both ways. Some social analysts have seen big-time football as a prime reinforcer of sexism.

Going to the stadium is seen not as an escape from the rest of life but as a pilgrimage to a shrine, where the virtues of toughness and insensitivity can be renewed. The code of toughness leads to the idea that if you are the strongest you should have your way. That kind of thinking led to Watergate. And, interestingly enough, Watergate was an all-male affair. Although it contradicted what is best in our democratic heritage, Watergate was in full accord with the old image of masculinity, with its quick trigger finger and glorification of violence. Too many men in our society are trapped into thinking that their sexual identity is somehow connected with an exaggerated aggression. Violence and sexism are closely related. "The young man is encouraged to 'score' with girls, to 'make' women. This is a sexuality of conquest, of trophies to deck out his ego."[11] The "macho" male mystique emphasizes individualistic self-aggrandizement through the domination of others. Our society has an enormous job to do in eliminating this ". . . learned pattern of relationships among men that creates an adversary and domineering style between male and male and toward all females."[12]

After writing the above paragraph, I went home to lunch and was given by my wife (ever watchful for items like this) a clipping from last night's paper reporting on the latest Gallup Youth Survey. It proves that I am not truly "with it" when I write as I did a few lines above about John Wayne. (This survey was taken before his death.) In answer to the question, "Who is your favorite movie personality?" boy teenagers chose first, guess who: John Wayne. Second, was Clint Eastwood and third, was Sylvester Stallone. All three are "macho" types. And two of these top three were in the top four choices of girls! The Liberation Movement has a lot of work to do![13]

The great fear of all men is of impotence. It does

not matter how successful he is anywhere else in life, if he cannot rise to the occasion when naked between the sheets, he does not consider himself a complete "man."

> Women are immeasurably lucky in this respect. A woman can never suffer this humiliating failure, can never really be in a state of being incapable of performing at least the movements of love.[14]

Psychologist Theodore Reik has said that "in our civilization women are afraid that they will be considered only women — and men are afraid that they will not be considered men enough."[15] And, thanks to the new freedom women have in demanding their rights, sexual as well as otherwise, men have a new worry added to their old one. Virility used to be thought of as a unilateral expression of male sexual competence. But now it means the ability to evoke a full sexual response from the female. "Many modern girls are becoming critical consumers of male performance,"[16] said David Riesman of Harvard. Many of us remember the list of males compiled by a group of coeds, which described in detail each one's sexual capabilities. It was like a consumer's guide to notable campus studs. In one sense it was a great case of finally getting even, but also it shows that it is a new and more difficult world for men. It is not as easy for a young man to achieve the basic self-confidence that is the basis for his virility. Males no longer have their private sanctuaries where they can take refuge from women. A startling illustration of the desexualization of so many formerly sexually segregated parts of life is the cover of the magazine *Wrestling Illustrated*. It now has under the title these words: "Combined with *Girl Wrestling.*"[17] A frigid woman does not consider her condition a sign that she has lost her womanhood, because it does not keep her from fulfilling a "performance" requirement. Some puritanical elements in society might even elevate her infirmity to the rank of a virtue.

> Whereas it is near to impossible to imagine any woman committing suicide because she was frigid, a significant percentage of men do commit suicide because they are impotent or think they are.[18]

Sex still remains more important to men than it is to women. In 1975 a psychologist, Paul Cameron, who was then in Maryland but is currently on the faculty of Fuller Theological Seminary in Pasadena, California, received national newspaper coverage about a survey he had taken. He asked 818 men and women to rank 22 daily activities in order of importance.

Men under 26 ranked music and sex #1 (a tie)
Men 26 to 39 ranked sex #1
Men 40 to 55 ranked family #1, nature and sex tied for #2
Men 56 to 64 ranked employment #1, sex and sports tied for #8
Men 65 and over ranked sex #15
Women: no age group ranked sex #1
Women under 26 ranked music, nature, family and travel ahead of sex
Women 26 to 39 ranked sex and job the same, #4 (after nature, family and music)
Women 40 to 55 ranked housework, sleep and TV all ahead of sex (family #1)
Women 56 to 65 ranked sex #13
Women 65 and over ranked sex #17

For both, greater sexual pleasure was reported by those with the highest level of education (sex is very connected with the head!). The income level did not relate to anything. So the old female cry, "All you men are ever interested in is sex," is right!

Young men have particular difficulty keeping their sexual drive under control, not just because they are in the period of life with the highest sex drive, but because they have not had enough experience to combat the normal cultural conditioning. A young male naturally picks up this kind of an idea of the male sex drive:

> It is very powerful and hard to control. In fact once it gets going it is very difficult to stop and really should not be thwarted. It is cruel for a woman to arouse a man and then cut him off.

This is, of course, just the opposite of what is true. Adult male sexuality is, for emotionally healthy men, a controllable activity with only minimal problems of control. Most men receive a significant part of their sexual satisfaction (emotionally) from giving their female partners pleasure, and controlling one's own response is an important means of achieving that end.

But it is admittedly a constant battle for many men to keep their sexuality loving and creative. The problem is complicated by the choice that both some men and some women make to use their sexuality to solve other personality problems. A woman may choose — much against her will or her better judgment — to make herself sexually available to a male, but that "choice" will often be so dominated by cultural and psychological factors operating at an unconscious level that it will not even feel to the woman like a choice. Men will frequently respond to such a woman out of similar needs of their own. At such points, sexual drive in both males and females becomes the vehicle for manipulation of each by the other. Since the motivation for such using of one another is usually kept out of conscious awareness, it is understandable (though not acceptable) if either men or women refer to a presumed uncontrollability of the sex drive, and if men attempt to place the responsibility for the initiative in seduction on women, or *vice versa*.

According to Dr. Melvin Anchell, nature made the male sex drive more intense for a very good reason. He writes,

> ... man's sexual desires are intensified if he has to overcome obstacles before achieving sexual communion with women ... women are more completely gratified with sexual intimacy only after a long wooing. Opposition heightens the intensity of any instinct. When the male receives stimulating opposition to his mating urge, he will then use his excess libidinal energies to create a more favorable situation ... the whole progress of human civilization depends upon the male's being thwarted to a natural extent in his mating instinct. When the female plays hard to get she is aiding in this process ... When she goes against nature and becomes a "free lover," the female destroys not only herself but the future of the civilization of which she is a vital part.[19]

That may seem to be a very extreme statement, but it does contain some truth. Sex is full of mysteries and dilemmas. Within it are found the tensions between purpose and pleasure, and

Control vs. Abandon,
Giving vs. Taking,
Physical vs. Emotional.

There is also the tension between the common biological sources of sexuality which are alike in all people, and the uniqueness of each individual that makes every person's sexuality totally distinctive. Each has his/her own sexuality and his/her own expression of that sexuality, and yet in all of us the sources of the variations are the same.

What Are the Facts About Male-Female Differences?

Are there any real differences between men and women beyond the obvious biological ones? Those who say there are *not* believe that the apparent differences are all the result of thousands of years of male-dominated culture. Also, there seems to be the belief among people of this persuasion that if there was any admission of innate differences, then these facts would almost automatically be used as evidence of the inferiority of the female; but it could just as easily result in saying the *male* is the inferior! The truth probably is that there are indeed differences between the sexes, but that these differences do not carry with them any value judgments; and that cultural conditioning has an enormous influence on how these differences are interpreted. For instance, Simone de Beauvoir writes about the menstrual cycle as

> a burden, and a useless one from the point of view of the individual . . . [Woman] feels her body most painfully as an obscure, alien thing . . . Woman, like man, *is* her body, but her body is something other than herself.[20]

Man, on the other hand, is thought of as superior because his sexual development is so much easier. But then you have an opposite opinion, again from a woman, Margaret Mead. She feels sorry for the men who, according to her, are

> faced with the unsure onset of puberty, the unsure status of paternity, and the unsure end of potency, [and] must compensate their insecurities by compensatory achievement. Women with their visible, immediate, productive, and defined sexual development have all the psychological advantage.[21]

So, interpretation is probably more important than the facts. But what are the facts?

Let us start at the embryo. Recent embryological research has shown that all human embryos are morphologically female in their early stage. Even if there is a Y chromosome present (which is what determines that it will eventually be a male)

> ... the human male begins to differentiate from the female by the action of fetal androgens; where these androgens are lacking, even genetic males will develop into females ... [It seems] that [a] foetus has to force its maleness on a body and brain which are only too inclined to choose the path to femininity.[22]

As the two sexes mature there are differences that appear to be based on structural, hormonal or neurological differences. Let us begin with the female: First, females are healthier than males.

> Nature obviously has a huge stake in keeping females healthy because, while human pregnancy lasts so long, it usually results in only a single helpless infant. Mothers have to adapt to unusual hormonal and anatomical changes during pregnancy and, in all but recent times, be healthy enough to suckle their young effectively for two or three years after if a wet nurse is not available.[23]

Second, females mature earlier than males. This is good for reproduction. They are more likely to give birth while still young and strong enough to care for the children.

Third, females cease ovulating (usually) in their late forties, while males remain potent. Nature obviously thinks late childbearing is too risky both for the mother and the child. And certainly, in the early part of human evolution, if a woman did survive she probably would not live long enough to care for a late child.

> By permitting older females to escape the hazards of childbirth, nature gave them a longer lease on life ... and caretaking resources are multiplied through aunts, grandmothers, midwives and female friends.[24]

Fourth, females

> do not seem to be driven to frequent sexual arousal and activity as early as males . . . there are anatomical and physiological reasons for the earlier sexuality of boys. Because the penis . . . lies outside the body, it is subject to frequent stimulation . . . Mothers have long observed that the penis is one of the small boy's first toys; and it has been found that normal young adult males have erect penises during more than half their dreaming time while asleep although the content of the dream probably is not sexual most of the time . . . Awareness of genital tumescence comes much later in females than males, perhaps as late as between eight and thirteen on the average. In addition, nature has arranged to give nearly all females a hymen in what Margaret Mead suggests was an effort to discourage early genitality.[25]

So nature seems to have planned for females to enjoy genital sex when they are older and when it would be difficult to disassociate sex from childbearing.

Now let us look at the male.

First, because of the phallic nature of his sex, males have an urge toward expansion in space. This is a

> tendency . . . to stake out and defend, and possibly to expand his own territory . . . [This] does not necessarily have to be an area localized in space; it may be . . . a particular field of work.[26]

Second, men are more aggressive than females and this is connected with, and makes possible, the first trait. It also tends toward a striving for superior status. "She prefers the center to the frontiers, the conservation and administration of what has already been secured, to the struggle for expansion."[27] Margaret Mead says it this way:

> In every known human society the male's need for achievement can be recognized . . . In a great number . . . men's sureness of their sex role is tied up with their right, or ability, to practice some activity that women are not allowed to practice. Their maleness, in fact, has to be underwritten by preventing women from entering some field or performing some feat. Here

may be found the relationship between maleness and pride . . . men do need to find reassurance in achievement, and because of this connection, cultures frequently phrase achievement as something that women do not or cannot do, rather than directly as something which we do well . . . Few cultures have yet found ways in which to give women a divine discontent that will demand other satisfactions than those of childbearing.[28]

Differences in General

An exhaustive study by two women in 1974 reviewed all the clinical data then available about sex differences. Some of the results were these:[29]

Girls are *not* more "social" than boys. Any differences that do exist in this area have to do with the "kind" of sociability the two sexes prefer. Boys are highly oriented toward a peer group, and congregate in larger groups. Girls associate in pairs or small groups, and may be somewhat more inclined toward adults.

Boys are *not* more "analytic" than girls. The sexes do not differ on tests of analytic cognitive style.

Girls *do* have greater verbal ability than boys.

Boys *do* have greater visual-spatial ability.

Boys *do* excel in mathematical ability, but the difference from the girls in this skill is not as great as it is in spatial ability.

Males *are* more aggressive than females. This difference is found as early as social play begins — at age two or two and one-half. It declines with age although the difference remains through the college years. Little information is available for older adults. Does this male predisposition toward aggression contribute to social dominance? The authors say,

> Probably yes, to some degree, but the case is not strong . . . However, there is no direct evidence that dominance among adult human groups is linked either to sex hormones or to aggressiveness. The fact that "dominance" in most human groups is called "leadership" provides a clue to the fact that

adult human beings influence one another by persuasion, charisma, mutual affection, and bargaining, as well as by force or threats thereof. To the extent that dominance is *not* exercised by coercion, the biological male aggressiveness is probably not implicated in it.[30]

The authors did agree that the sex difference in aggression does have a biological foundation. "Aggression is related to levels of sex hormones, and can be changed by experimental administrations of these hormones."[31] I quote these words because they relate to another interesting book, *The Inevitability of Patriarchy,* by Steven Goldberg. His views are these:

> No anthropologist contests the fact that patriarchy is universal. Indeed, of all social institutions there is probably none whose universality is so totally agreed upon . . . Anthropologists debate problems of definition and borderline cases. [But] There is not, nor has there ever been, any society that even remotely failed to associate authority and leadership in suprafamilial areas with the male.[32]

> The arguments of the feminists are these: There is nothing inherent in the nature of human beings or of society that necessitates that any role or task (save those requiring great strength or the ability to give birth) be associated with one sex or the other; there is no natural order of things decreeing that dyadic and social authority must be associated with men . . . Patriarchy, matriarchy, and "equiarchy" are all equally possible and . . . all the expectations we have of men and women are culturally determined and have nothing to do with any sort of basic male or female nature.[33]

Goldberg cites the fact that males have more testosterone than females, and that this hormone is directly related to aggression. This male "advantage" in aggression, he believes, renders patriarchy and male dominance inevitable and explains the anthropological findings:

> . . . the central fact is that men and women are different from each other from gene to the thought to the act and that emotions that underpin masculinity and femininity, that make

reality as experienced by the male eternally different from that experienced by the female, flow from the biological natures of man and woman. This is the one fact that the feminist cannot admit. For to admit this would be to admit that the liberations of men and women must proceed along different and complementary lines...[34]

About all this Maccoby and Jacklin answer:

It has been alleged [ref. to Goldberg] that aggression is the primary means whereby human beings dominate one another, so that in cross-sex encounters it will be true that (with rare exceptions) men will dominate women, and will therefore come to occupy the positions in society in which status and authority are vested... We believe it is true that males have occupied the high status positions in the large majority of human social groupings through the history of man. We do not think this is an historical accident. We doubt, however, that dominance and leadership are inevitably linked to aggression. Aggression may be the primary means by which apes and little boys dominate one another... However, aggression is certainly not the method most usually employed for leadership among mature human beings... We must leave it to the reader's judgment to estimate how often the "killer instinct" is involved in achieving success in the business or political world. Clearly it sometimes is, and in these cases there will be a smaller number of women than men who will have the temperament for it. We wish only to suggest that it is entirely possible to achieve status by other means, and that the sexes have a more equal chance at success by these alternative routes.[35]

As things stand today the male is undoubtedly the more aggressive. He is the primary perpetrator of violent crimes. The National Commission on Violence reported in 1969 that violent crime in the city is overwhelmingly committed by males. "In 1968 the homicide rate was five times greater for males; for robbery it was twenty times higher."[36] All through history, males have committed more of all types of crime, with the obvious exception of strictly female crimes like abortion. Later statistics have been alarming in the great rate of increase in female crimes. But it does not look as if the male will lose his lead.

What About Sexual Differences?

Helmut Thielicke in his book, *The Ethics of Sex*, presents very well the traditional Western approach to sexual differences. He writes,

> ... the woman is identified with her sexuality quite differently from the man. It is, so to speak, the "vocation" of the woman to be lover, companion, and mother. And even the unmarried woman fulfills her calling in accord with the essential image of herself only when these fundamental characteristics . . . undergo a sublimating transformation but still remain discernible; that is to say, when love and motherliness are the sustaining forces in her vocation. The man, on the other hand, invests a much smaller quantum of the substance of his being in the sex community. He has totally different tasks and aims beyond the sex relationship . . . [the] outside world claims a far larger part of his time. The nature of man . . . comes out more strongly in confrontation with what Schiller called "hostile life," in which he must struggle, take risks, scheme, and hunt. Therefore the wife gives her "self" when she gives herself sexually. She holds nothing back, and precisely in doing this she comes to her self-realization . . . Whereas the husband brings in only a part, a very substantial part but still only a part, of himself . . . [so] the man is not nearly so deeply stamped and molded by his sexual experience as is the case with the woman . . . . In the physiological structure of the sex organs: whereas the woman receives something into herself, the male sex organ is directed outward, away from himself; it discharges. The *receiving* of something is contrasted with being *relieved* of something . . . The extraordinary force of the symbolism of this disparate physical structure can hardly be evaded.[37]

How do you feel about the above statement? Sounds a little old-fashioned, does it not? Maybe not. But for some it may seem to be too rigid in its assigning an entire life style of nurturing to anyone with a female body. It also gives the impression that males have more important things to do than be involved in sexuality; almost as if a male's sexuality is a negative thing within him that builds up and occasionally has to be discharged. Here is a slightly different approach to sexual differences:

> The male is the one who is more responsive to visual and narrative stimulation, and the female is more responsive to the sentimental and romantic type of stimulation . . . If a woman sees a sexy picture, for instance, even an advertisement for Coco-Cola, she tends to project herself up onto the screen, onto the picture, and to imagine what it would be like to be that woman. Or if she's seeing a sexy film, or a romantic film, to project herself into the story and perhaps change it a little to suit certain circumstances of her own existence, and also to feel that she's learning a few good lessons from the woman up there. She will then be able to put the lessons into practice in her own romantic and sexual life. As for the male viewer, his reaction is rather different, for he does not project himself up into the picture of a male on the screen and imagine what it would be like to be that lucky one with that good looking girl. He objectifies. He takes the girl down off the screen and has sex with her on the spot.[38]

Here we have a more contemporary way of saying that there are distinct differences in the attitudes and emotional responses of men and women to sexual stimulation. The reader must remember, of course, that we do not mean to imply that all men and all women fit neatly into any descriptions of males "in general" or females "in general." Every individual is a totally unique example of a sexual person. Many males are more "feminine" than many females and vice versa. Some men demand emotional involvement for sexual satisfaction and some women can enjoy themselves sexually without emotional involvement. But the extreme variations among individuals do not mean that we should be deterred from trying to understand group norms and general patterns within the two types of sexual persons. Unless the Women's Liberation Movement has completely revised our concepts of sex differences, we can still say that for (the majority of) males, sexual desire arises much more spontaneously than it does for (the majority of) females. For men, it may occur in the absence of any emotional stimulation. Women are much more dependent on some form of erotic stimulation in the form of emotional warmth or physical caressing. A woman's emotions are much more closely connected with her sexuality than is true for men.

> Sexual intercourse for sexual pleasure alone is much less appealing to a woman than to a man. A woman requires that everything should be in keeping with her feelings and with those of her lover. A man is much less exacting about the setting of the sexual act.[39]

Here is an interesting attempt to tie together and explain these big emotional and attitudinal differences in the sexes with the obvious bodily differences:

> Since the woman's sexuality is diffused and internalized throughout her entire body, the man finds the woman's entire body a sexual attraction. But since the man's sexuality is localized and externalized the woman does not as easily interpret the man's body, merely as a body, as a sexual stimulus. She is attracted to his *person* and is aroused more by the whole context of the loving situation than by mere sight or contact, as such, with the man's body. When the man's bodily gestures express deep personal affection, the *meaning* of these kisses and caresses touches her soul and awakens her body to physical desire. The woman attracts the man to her person through her body; the man awakens the woman to his body through his person.[40]

Which sex gains the most satisfaction in the sexual act? This is an age-old question, and obviously a true comparison is impossible. The only person who was ever thought capable of so judging was the mythical Tiresias. According to legend, he had been turned into a woman, but eventually regained his masculine body. It seems that Hera, the Olympian queen of heaven and goddess of women and marriage, was complaining to Zeus, her husband, for one of Zeus's many infidelities. He told her not to complain since as a woman she gained far more pleasure when they did have intercourse. Hera did not accept Zeus's infinite knowledge, and came back with the fact that everyone knew that the man gained more pleasure from the act than the woman. To resolve the quarrel they called in Tiresias, and admitted that for once a mortal could know something hidden even from a god. Tiresias stated that if the pleasure of the sexual act could be divided into ten parts, nine parts would belong to the woman. This assertion angered Hera so much that she struck Tiresias blind.[41]

It is an interesting tale. Why should the wife in the story be so angered by the idea that she received a lot more sexual pleasure than her husband? Because that would justify his seeking variety and quantity since he could not enjoy the same quality? Or was her anger a cover-up for her fear, fear for herself? Perhaps she was not having that much pleasure, and she did not like the idea of experiencing that much more pleasure for fear that she might become addicted to it. Or, had this fact been a perfectly kept feminine secret, and Hera was furious that Tiresias had revealed it to the males?

There is a modern version of the problem that might be implied in this old myth. Some writers in the Women's Liberation Movement believe that there are truths about female sexual pleasure that we are just beginning to understand. According to a psychiatrist and researcher in sexuality, Mary Jane Sherfey, female sexuality was, in prehistoric times, an insatiable physical drive that has been powerfully repressed for the sake of orderly human relations. She writes:

> There are many indications from prehistory studies in the Near East that it took perhaps 5,000 years or longer for the subjugation of women to take place. All relevant data from the 12,000-to-8,000 B.C. period indicates that precivilized woman enjoyed full sexual freedom and was often totally incapable of controlling her sexual drive . . . [there was at that time an] intense, insatiable eroticism in women.[42]
>
> Not until these drives were gradually brought under control by

> rigidly enforced social codes could family life become the stabilizing and creative crucible from which modern civilized man could emerge.[43]

According to this writer, woman's clitoris is the source of all the pleasure and all the problems. It is the only organ whose sole function is to provide pleasure. Penis and vagina are both designed for the act of impregnation, and the penis also serves to contain the channel for urination. The clitoris is also unique in that it is not subject to the cycle or rapid detumescence and gradual recovery that limits the penis. So the theory is that during this pre-historical period women were consumed by the drive for sexual pleasure, and the only thing that every stopped them was simple fatigue. This, of course, could not go on if anything else was to get accomplished so, according to the theory, men succeeded in inventing various ways of forcing women to forget about their natural orgasmic birthright. The real fear in males, of course, was not being needed. According to one recent writer:

> Men fear that they will become sexually expendable if the clitoris is substituted for the vagina as the center of pleasure for women . . . Lesbian sexuality could make an excellent case, based on anatomical data, for the extinction of the male organ.[44]

Freud is cited as a major source of the contemporary problem. He believed that clitoral orgasm was an expression of immaturity, neuroticism, masculinity, and/or frigidity, and that to become completely feminine a woman must be able to have the better type of orgasm located in the vagina. Then came Kinsey. He showed that there was a very great range of sexual experience among women — much greater than that for men. Some women reported having many orgasms within a few moments. He also had statistics on women who said they had fifty orgasms in a single month. Next, we have Masters and Johnson. Their observations and interviews with 487 women discovered

> ... that the dichotomy of vaginal and clitoral orgasms is entirely false. Anatomically, all orgasms are centered in the clitoris ... [And that] women are naturally multi-orgasmic; that is, if a woman is immediately stimulated following orgasm, she is likely to experience several orgasms in rapid succession.[45]

Later, Masters and Johnson reported that women can have fifty orgasms in an hour through clitoral-area stimulation. So attitudes have changed! With the old understanding, a woman's pleasure was obtained through the vagina, which meant she was totally dependent on the male, and she would receive her satisfaction only as a concomitant of man's seeking his. With the center of the pleasure having shifted, women's sexual pleasure becomes possibly independent of the male's pleasure. The dean of American pastoral counsellors, Seward Hiltner, was fantasizing about where this might lead. He wrote:

> ... most women (unless impeded by specific disease or restrained by social standards) have the capacity for far more orgasms than even the prize male stud can claim ... I have been trying to imagine what a "pan-sexualist" utopia would be like if absolutely all taboos on sexual activity were removed except those involving injury, exploitation, coercion, and the like. If females had the psychic inclination to realize their full orgasmic potentialities, then there would have to be sexual acts between females, and these would far outnumber all heterosexual acts and all male homosexual acts combined! For any woman physically tuned up to use all her capabilities for orgasm all the time, sexual relations with men would become comparatively speaking, "breaks" in the "normative" female-to-female pattern ... Is it not likely that ... women guided by instinct and pleasure alone could cause far more havoc than men motivated by the same factors?[46]

Yes, the sexes are sexually very different. But is it not interesting that the God who made us this way, and called it "good" gave the males, who tend to be ready for sexual activity all the time, equipment that has some built-in limits. But to the females, who tend to be much less interested all the time, he gave equipment that hardly has any limits at all! I think we can depend on the "natural" desire for relationship and meaning, for love and commitment to continue to accompany and dominate female sexual acts. It is that desire which will keep females from becoming simple pursuers of pleasure.

Some Further Thoughts About Male-Female Differences

Males and females are different. The depth of the difference seems inexhaustible, and yet in the unity which comes from combining the diversity, there arises a mysterious and wondrous new intensity of life for both. This harmony symbolizes the reconciliation of all of life's opposites: body-soul, conscious-unconscious, dependence-independence, reason-emotion, and so on. It is called complementarity.

Women who have been influenced by the Women's Liberation Movement often do not like the concept of complementarity. For many of them it means the acceptance of a basic and fundamental difference between the sexes. Too often "difference" seems to inevitably connote inequality. The fear is that if you are different you must be either inferior to or superior to the one with whom you contrast. For that reason many women want to avoid any concepts of complementarity. They feel it inevitably leads to another "put-down." But true complementarity can only exist between equals. The fear is understandable but the remedy is much worse than the disease. To deny or even to play down the differences between the sexes is to weaken the structure from which arises the love that can be experienced between men and women. I'm not saying that all love is thus crippled, but a basic type is: that is the erotic.

Eros is an important type of love. It is not as altruistic as Agape (willed concern for the best welfare of the other), and it is not as comfortable as Philia (the attraction between people who are alike), but it is more dynamic than either because it is based on the polarity and tensions created by male-female differences. The two sexes are designed to need each other. The individual sex organ is wondrously fashioned so as not to be satisfied with itself but to long for its completion in another. Part of that longing is based on the delight of its being so totally different from the other that it can provide what is needed for the other's completion. Eros is based on difference. It is the need of incomplete and radically different beings for each other that makes the love so powerful and fulfilling. It is difficult not to shudder when a woman says she would rather be known as a person than as a woman. A primary way one becomes a person is through the process of interacting in multifarious ways with that mysterious other half of the human race. They are an "other half" because they are indeed "other" than yourself. The term "person" can easily imply a being that is somehow complete, static, secure, independent. But we are not this way. We are all like God. Even God is not a lonely isolated entity. God is Tri-unity, three in relation. We are most like God when we are in relationship with an "other." The fundamental element in a person that enables him/her to be a "being-in-relationship" is that "him/herness;" the difference in sexes. It is indeed mysterious how we become individuals by giving ourselves away to another. Sexual differences are one of the great helps we have from God to nudge us ever onward toward the "other." Sex is mysterious, and what it can do for us is mysterious.

Our sexuality will not let us rest in simply "being." It complements our basic isolation and lures us out of ourselves to the other who is "different." Let us never stop celebrating that God-given difference in complementarity.

5
Pre-Marital Sexuality

Any discussion of pre-marital sexuality will be difficult because of the powerful emotions this topic arouses. As we remember our own late adolescence, most of us have conflicting feelings. Very few of us went through that time in an ideal way. For the rest of us there are guilts about how we handled certain aspects of our lives, and at the same time we also may have no little pride in having done what we look back on as the right thing in certain circumstances. We remember the fears and confusions and ignorances which we often repressed and sometimes hardly recognized. It was tough. And yet, we remember the great excitement of maturing, of establishing identity and new, deeper relationships with others, of being on our own for the first time, and yet for many of us, we still did not have the burdens of serious responsibilities. It was great fun. In one respect it was a time we are glad we never will have to live through again. In another, it will always seem to have been a golden, escapist time-out vacation from the rest of life. It was bad; it was good. So when we try to understand the sexual lives of this age group today, we will bring to our study powerful biases of our own.

For some of us, there is a more recent cause for even further anxiety connected with this topic: we have some dearly loved people, sons and daughters, who are living through or who have made it through this period in their lives. We are as emotionally involved in their struggles and joys as we were in our own. How to be a good parent to an adolescent is just as problematic a job as being the adolescent. "Are we doing the right thing?" is almost a daily question. Here, as in most things, we have prides and guilts. All we can do about these powerful and conflicting emotions is to be aware of them and include them in the discussion. Sometimes they will help. Other times they will hurt, but always they will add reality and new life to the process.

The Social Situation

Someone has described the recent change in our society as a "sexplosion." Ours may be the most sex-saturated culture the world has ever seen. Sex has become combined with the profit motive. It helps to sell almost everything, and personally, too many of us are brainwashed into believing that being sexually desirable is the most important single aspect of human life. Twenty years ago there were few women who would not be offended if you called them "sexy." Today, almost everyone, men included, delights to hear such a compliment. You might call it a sex-starved culture. Starved for real sexual involvement because it is so saturated with superficial, phony, loveless sex.

It is hard to determine exactly how this sexplosion has affected sexual behavior. There have been a lot of small surveys, but little has been done to up-date the large scale work of the Kinsey Report.

The best recent poll of young people I know of was published in 1973 by Robert C. Sorensen: *Adolescent Sexuality in Contemporary America*. This was a survey by mail and private interviews (c. 200) of about 400 teen-agers (from thirteen to nineteen years old) out of the total U.S. population of twenty-seven million teen-agers. Some of the results are as follows:

Forty-eight percent claim to be virgins.

Fifty-two percent have had intercourse (fifty-nine

percent of the boys, forty-five percent of the girls).

Twenty-five percent of the boys had their first intercourse with a girl they met only shortly before.

Thirty-six percent of the girls had first intercourse with a boy they planned to marry.

Fifty-five percent said neither partner used birth control in first intercourse. Another twenty-three percent were not sure.

Forty percent had had first intercourse in their own or their partner's home.

Fear is the reaction that girls most frequently report after their first intercourse (sixty-three percent). However, only twenty-three percent of the boys were aware of this.

Excitement is the immediate reaction to first intercourse most frequently reported by boys (forty-six percent).

Forty-one percent of all non-virgin adolescents believe God has no interest in their sex life; although fifty percent say they sometimes worry whether God would approve of their sexual behavior.

Seventy-four percent of all adolescents agree that too many young people these days are irresponsible where sex is concerned.

Three-fifths of all boys and nearly one-fifth of all girls with intercourse experience believe it is all right for someone to have intercourse with another person he/she has known only a few hours.[1]

As this is being written, the latest TIME magazine (October 8, 1979) has a brief article (on page 10) on a new and even larger survey of 625 teenagers by Aaron Hass, entitled, *Teenage Sexuality*, published by Macmillan. It claims that among fifteen to sixteen year-olds, forty-three percent of the boys and thirty-one percent of the girls have had intercourse. About twenty-eight percent of the boys in the same age range have had ten or more sexual partners. The same is true of seven percent of the girls.

We do know that the "pill" has played a very minor role in pre-marital sexual behavior of adolescents or of the college population. In the majority of cases, first intercourse has taken place without the use of any contraceptives whatever and only a very small minority have used the pill.[2] The most recent Kinsey Report (1968) of first coitus on the college campus indicated an increase of perhaps twenty-five percent in pre-marital intercourse over the original Kinsey sample[3] (that original statistic was that, in 1948, forty-eight percent of men from sixteen to twenty-five who went beyond the twelfth grade engaged in coitus at least occasionally). There are also indications that there has been little change in the enormous differences between how males and females view the person with whom they first have intercourse: "Females surrender their virginity to males they love whereas males are much less emotionally involved."[4] The average age at which intercourse begins has changed very little, and for college males prostitution has become insignificant as a source of initial intercourse. There are few indications that female promiscuity has become more common. Most sexual activity for girls still occurs within the context of affection and impending marriage, and boys seem to be moving away from greater promiscuity toward the same norm as the females. The big revolution has obviously taken place in openness. Also to be noted are the decline of the influence of the family and the growing assumption of responsibility by young people for their own sexual behavior.[5] Since the voting age was dropped to eighteen, colleges and universities have felt unresponsible for the sexual behavior of these "adults." Few institutions still try to be "in loco parentis."

The Bible and Pre-Marital Sexuality

Old Testament religion is a religion of and for men. It was pre-eminently a successful patriarchy. In ancient Israel the female is not regarded as quite equal to the male. In fact she is thought of as his property. Adultery is wrong partly because it is a form of stealing from another man. It was not thought of as injuring the wife, only her owner. So intercourse with a woman before she is married mainly affects her desirability as a potential mate. Pre-marital intercourse between betrothed couples does not seem to have been regarded as scandalous. According to the *Mishnah,* the authoritative collection of Jewish Oral Law, it was one of the three recognized ways of effecting a betrothal. Nothing in the Bible, Old or New Testaments, explicitly forbids pre-marital sexual acts, although it can be inferred from St. Paul's idea that to have intercourse with anyone, at anytime, is to become "one-flesh" with that person.[6] So, according to St. Paul, there really is no such thing as pre-marital intercourse, since the intercourse itself makes the relationship marital.

Bishop John A. T. Robinson, in his book, *The Human Face of God,* presents a startling idea: that Jesus himself was the result of pre-marital intercourse. If you believe in the Virgin Birth literally then his logic is not something you can follow with acceptance, but if you, with many other sincere Christians, believe that doctrine to be of symbolic importance (meaning it is an important way of conveying the *meaning* that the Incarnation was an act that God initiated, not man), then he raises some interesting problems. He first asks us to decide how Mary conceived. There are three possibilities:
1. Conception and birth in wedlock,
2. Conception by Joseph outside wedlock,

subsequently legitimized, and
3. Conception outside wedlock, by an unknown party, subsequently legitimized by Joseph.

Of these three possibilities:
1. has no New Testament evidence to support it at all,
2. is specifically denied by Matthew 1:18, and
3. is obviously the most embarrassing alternative, and one that early Christians would be most concerned to repudiate. Some commentators hear this charge being leveled at Jesus in two passages: Mark 6:3 "son of Mary" and John 8:41 "We are not illegitimate!" (implying you are. Emphasis mine). The most interesting thing about all this is the line of defense against this slander that Matthew takes in his gospel. When he writes the long list of people in the lineage of Jesus he does not seem at all disturbed by the difficulty involved if Joseph was not the genetic father. In fact, he seems to want to emphasize it, as if to say that God is used to working through the unusual. He does this by going out of his way to prove that God has done this sort of thing before. As proof, he adds to his list four women. No women appear in Luke's list. That would be odd enough in itself but these four are unusual women. "The one thing they apparently have in common is the dubiety of their sexual liaisons."[7] Then, as the fifth, comes Mary. It is as if Matthew was not trying to deny the irregularities, but rather trying to tell us between the lines that the heir had often been born out of the direct line or irregularly, and that it is all entirely compatible with Jesus being the Messiah from God.

The ethic Jesus taught was based on love. "I give you a new commandment: love one another; just as I have loved you, you also must love one another." (John 13:34) The new thing about this commandment is the new example of love, the life of Christ himself.

"Love, for him, meant not primarily a romantic emotion, but concern and respect, devotion and desire to serve."[8] We are to imitate Christ in his freedom, his faith, his integrity, his responsibility and concern for people. This norm of Christ-like love is to be sought in inner attitudes and motives. Jesus always recognized the unique status of the person as over against a legalism which ignores the individual. Does this mean that Jesus would condone the sexual relations of a couple who genuinely love each other, but are not married? There are those who would say yes, and hold the position that Jesus' sole concern was for motivation without regard to social conditions or mores. Others would say no, and ask why the couple has decided not to be married. If in their own eyes they are married, they are committed, and the only difference in their marriage and others is that they have by-passed the social formalities, then yes, the church has always recognized common law marriages. But if there is no "marriage" in either open or secret agreement, then these people would say, no, it cannot be seen as following Christ.

The Sacramental View

To believe in sacraments is to think that the spiritual part of life and the material part of life are both inseparably connected. Matter is for one purpose only: to convey spirit. This belief also involves the idea that there is naturally a certain appropriateness about the way particular "spirits" use certain kinds of matter. Hate expresses itself through cold steel, not balloons. So the sacramental understanding of human love believes that it is best conveyed through the materiality of our bodies: through sexuality. The appropriate material expression of the highest form of love between a man and a woman (which means total commitment to the other's best welfare) is sexual intercourse. It is the perfect way of doing something about that ultimate commitment.

Now, what about using that action (that outward and visible sign) to express something spiritual that is less than total commitment? Does that kind of an action hurt, or diminish, or confuse the relationship between intercourse and total commitment which people might want to make at some future time? It would seem reasonable to suppose so. The process of changing the spiritual meaning connected with some matter or action while not changing the latter is problematical. Imagine a man who works in a fish food manufacturing company which makes the old style white sheets of fish food which used to be crumbled in pieces and dropped into aquariums. His job is that of tasting the fish food to be sure its quality remains high. Let us say this man decides to become an Episcopalian. He takes confirmation instruction and is told how to receive Communion and what Communion means. He believes quite strongly that Jesus Christ makes his spiritual presence real through the matter of bread and wine. But when this man receives his first communion, he finds it is extremely difficult to realize the spiritual aspect of this sacrament because when he is given his wafer it seems so much like the fish food that he samples every day.

The same point is made in a secular way by Rustum and Della Roy in their book, *Honest Sex:*

> Sex may be likened to a pen. A pen is, of course, performing its designed function and maximum capability when it is used as a means of writing. But pens may also be used to scratch backs or tickle ears or dig the cement out of cracks in the desk or punch holes in paper. Obviously, pens can be put to some secondary uses which are not at all destructive of the capacity of the pen to serve its primary purpose of an instrument of communication. But, digging out cement *may* clog even the newest ball points, and hence there are other uses of a pen

> which can destroy its primary function. We are sure that exploitive sex destroys its primary function; we believe that for most Christians today, impersonal sex becomes exploitive sex which warps or deadens our sensitivities and so impairs our ability to use it as the deepest expression of love between man and woman.[9]

Love must have a means of expressing itself which is appropriate to the love. Therefore, the greatest love should have the greatest act for its expression. Both need each other in order to be fully "real" in this sacramental world.

Some Contemporary Views

Humanists

The views of Humanists often come very close to those of Christians when they choose concern for personal values as their ethical norm. "Love thy neighbor as thyself" does not have to have any theistic referent. Professor Lester Kirkendall, probably the most knowledgeable humanist expert on pre-marital sexuality, has said:

> The essence of morality lies in the quality of interrelationships which can be established among people. Moral conduct is that kind of behavior which enables people in their relationships with each other to experience a greater sense of trust, and appreciation for others; which increases the capacity of people to work together; which reduces social distance and continually furthers one's outreach to other persons and groups; which increases one's sense of self-respect and produces a greater measure of personal harmony... Immoral behavior is just the converse.[10]

Fletcher comments:

> On this view, sarcasm and graft are immoral, but not sexual intercourse unless it is malicious or callous or cruel. On this

basis, an act is not wrong because of the act itself but because of its *meaning* — its motive and message.[11]

In Kirkendall's significant book, *Premarital Intercourse and Interpersonal Relations* (a sociological appraisal of 200 case studies of pre-marital intercourse), he says,

> Some deeply affectionate unmarried couples have, through the investment of time and mutual devotion, built a relationship which is significant to them, and . . . experience intercourse without damage to their total relationship . . . it seems that in practically all instances, "non-damaging" intercourse occurred in relationships which were already so strong in their own right that intercourse did not have much to offer toward strengthening them.[12]

Situation Ethics or the New Morality

Dr. Joseph Fletcher is the source of this often misunderstood version of Christian morality. Simply stated, it is not an attempt to do away with all rules. Rather, it is a way of looking at all ethical rules as attempts to be concrete about the single and only always-applicable rule for Christians which is to do the most loving thing. Jesus is the best example of that life-style. All good rules can be guidelines, but they can never be absolutes. Only love is the absolute, and that must always be actualized in the situation. About pre-marital intercourse, Dr. Fletcher writes:

> . . . there are two distinct questions to ask ourselves. One is: Should we prohibit and condemn premarital sex? The other is: Should we approve of it? To the first one I promptly reply in the negative. To the second I propose an equivocal answer, "Yes and no — depending on each particular situation."[13]

If decisions like this are made for you by some external authority, or if you make them in advance, then they will not be really *your* existential choices. They will not be your application of your ideals through your involvement. They will not be truly free and therefore could not be fully moral.

The Social Sciences

In recent years psychology has gained a new understanding of anxiety. Personal and social standards are now seen to be compromise formations in our attempts to manage anxiety. The anxiety from sexuality comes not simply from the confusion as to what to do with sexual organs, but how best we can deal with the anxiety that comes from being humans who have drives for both reproduction and tenderness. Among the young there is often the feeling that all sexual anxiety comes from these old people who tell us not to do something. That is simply projecting the source of their problems away from themselves onto someone else. Pre-marital intercourse can be seen as an indication of failure to manage anxiety. The American theologian Nels Ferre, when a graduate student at Harvard, asked the famous philosopher, Alfred North Whitehead, "How would you characterize reality, in one sentence?" Ferre said that the great man was taken aback at such a boyish question, but after a few minutes he answered it in six words: "It matters, and it has consequences."[14] That is why anxiety is such a common part of daily life. And, of course, the younger one is, the more difficult it is to gracefully respond to anxiety. Emotional maturity enables one to handle anxiety better. Dr. Theodore Lidz, in his respected book on human development, *The Person,* says he thinks emotional immaturity is more the source of sexual difficulties for young people than are questions of morals or ethics.[15]

Adolescents of both sexes tend to engage in sexual

relationships of either a transitory or more involved nature before they are ready... When a young couple has a sexual relationship, one member is apt to invest more of the self in it than the other, and not be able to accept the other's casualness; or when the affair is serious, one will be hurt when it breaks up, despite promises that neither would expect it to be permanent. Actual sexual difficulties are apt to occur more commonly among adolescents who are still not properly disengaged from their oedipal attachments, and who cannot cope with the dependency needs of a partner when they are far from being independent themselves. Of course, similar problems occur in young married couples. It is not a matter of age but of readiness, and couples are more apt to be ready when they must also consider the lifelong involvements of marriage. The solutions are not readily available, for there cannot be generalized answers. Here we are simply noting that the adolescent often considers such matters in terms of standards of morality and propriety, which they are willing to change, when questions of maturity may be more pertinent.[16]

Vance Packard, author of *The Sexual Wilderness*, wrote an article about a psychologist, Robert McMurry, who thinks that emotional maturity is the crucial problem for young people experimenting with intimacy. McMurry said we start out life being utterly immature emotionally:

but as we grow older, if we are lucky, we shed our childish immaturities and achieve emotional maturity. He wrote on a blackboard nine traits common to people who have not yet outgrown the emotional immaturity characteristic of pre-adult life: Selfishness, pleasure-mindedness, disregard for consequences, lack of self-discipline, show-off tendencies, destructiveness, refusal to accept responsibility, wishful thinking, and dependency.[17]

Packard adds his own comments:

At least the first eight of these traits are commonly present as motivating factors in the sexual experimentation of unsupervised adolescents. It seems reasonable that society insist that sexual intercourse be out-of-bounds for unmarried teen-agers, and when such acts occur they should be forcefully disapproved.[18]

A New Look at Virginity

Herbert W. Richardson, a Canadian theologian, has presented a new way of understanding virginity in two publications: the first, an article in *The Religious Situation — 1969* and then a more complete book-length treatment in *Nun, Witch, Playmate*. Richardson says that man has evolved sexually just as much as he has evolved biologically. He believes that one can look back on human history and see at crucial turning points in the evolution of human consciousness a distinct attitude toward virginity which reflects these changes and serves to promote them.

> Changes in consciousness give rise to changes in sexual behavior precisely because every consciousness includes a characteristic self-awareness. So the way in which man is aware of his world determines his way of being aware of himself and those sexual possibilities open to him.[19]

Richardson begins with the period before 7000 B.C. which he labels "mimetic consciousness." During this period, man's life imitated the biological processes in the surrounding environment. This is the "tribal" stage of human life. Man thinks of himself as a part of nature, and he experiences his own sexuality as part of the natural process of fecundity around him.

> In the tribe, woman held a position of coeminence with the man. In and through her motherhood, his biological life was continued. Man's "immortality" therefore depended upon woman. Through her fertility the ongoing life of the tribe was insured.[20]

The second period is from 7000 to 1000 B.C.: "ego consciousness." In this period, man makes the transition from preoccupation with biological power to a concern for legal power; from concern with fertility to concern with voluntary activity; from living in a kinship tribal society to living in a town or city. Abraham's move (Genesis 12:1f) is an illustration of this new consciousness. Here, man is freeing himself from total immersion in the cycle of nature and creating a life of his own through his own will. Man has discovered a second power within himself. The first was sex; the second is his own ego. This involved the displacement of the mother from her former position of equality with the father. Now the symbol of authority is the "King," the solitary male who incarnates the new power of the ego in himself. In the Bible, we can see the transition from biological-tribal to volitional-urban society. The understanding of God reflects this: The Old Testament God can be creative by the power of his will alone. It is this power to create without a partner that is the key to biblical monotheism. In this period of ego consciousness, the economic, political, legal and religious spheres of life are separated from the family. So men monopolize the leadership roles. Women, confined to the family, become subordinate to men. But in order to maintain this new consciousness there has to be a constant struggle against regressing into the old. Woman was seen as the source of the old instinctual sexuality and therefore had to be fought against. The highest social status was occupied by the all-male group.

> The consequence of this social evolution is that the position of Western women has been much lower than the position of women in Oriental societies. The compensating "gain" (if one so chooses to call it) is that Western man has become more highly individuated, or "ego conscious" . . . [But] this has involved him in a struggle against his own mimetic (tribal) consciousness and instinctual sexuality. This is what has made man's relation to his own sexuality a peculiarly difficult problem for the west.[21]

How did sexuality become affected? The key to membership in the important male groups was the practice of male virginity. Sexual intercourse was obviously not absolutely renounced. By virginity we mean, in this context, the discipline of segmenting sex, and at times and in certain situations being able to renounce it for limited periods. This way, men struggled together against their fear of dependence upon the female. They also helped each other through ritual war to fight that other great fear, death. The two fears of Womb and Tomb united the male group. This is why in ancient Israel there was the requirement that every male avoid the female during the time of war, and why the warrior Uriah refused to sleep with his wife, Bathsheba, even at the King's command. Male virginity proved competence in the ability to segment a sphere of voluntary behavior off from the sphere of instinctual bodily behavior. "Ego consciousness only emerges after the 'purely sensuous' has been repudiated through an act of human will."[22] To summarize this second stage in sexual evolution, Richardson would say: the ego consciousness requires the segmentalization of sex which is learned in the all-male group.

The third period had its beginning from 800 to 400 B.C. and is called "rational consciousness." The Buddha, Zoroaster, the Hebrew prophets, and the Greek philosophers all emerged in this amazing period of human history. They all saw a new thing. They became aware of a Transcendent Reality, beyond and behind both the biological processes, and the human will. This higher kind of life was not subject to change and decay. Humans experienced it as Spirit, or Eternal Reason or unchangeable Truth. A new capacity emerged with man's consciousness: the ability to withhold oneself from action in order to think, to contemplate. Man becomes a reasoning creature with the ability to be objective. The "will" which formerly was in the center of man's life now must give place to "reason." The rationally conscious person believes that behind everyday life is a universal spiritual life in which he participates. It is his participation in this spiritual life that makes the rationally conscious man feel that he becomes his true self. He renounces his private preferences in order to be at one with abstract truth. Sexually, this means that there enters onto the stage of history the ideal of perpetual virginity. It is based on a new kind of human consciousness, wherein a man no longer identifies with and feels the instinctual sexuality of his body as truly his own. Fulfillment is sought through a union with an eternal transcendent order, so sex is accidental rather than essential. Man's happiness is now seen to lie in the religious community of saints. The commitment to perpetual virginity becomes a symbol that what is ultimately real is an unchanging spiritual order. Renounced is that kind of love which has sexual orgasms and procreation as its purpose. This means that man now loves in a different way. The highest love has become the love of the soul in the body. This made possible the spiritual love between men and women. They could, for the first time become "friends," since friendship presupposes full equality and likeness. In this love, sexual differences were transcended in this "higher" communion. It was in early Christianity that this new rational consciousness came to its fullest expression. The renunciation of sexual life was the foundation of the new primary social group — the monastery. For the first time virginity was thought of as something for women as well as men. To summarize this third stage: the rational consciousness requires the renunciation of sex which is learned in monastic training.

    The fourth period called "self-consciousness," had its beginnings from 1300 to 1700 A.D. Here began the changes that eventually produced our modern technological culture. The great new idea this time was the belief that "... man ... himself might recreate the world of nature to accord with a vision of his own imagination."[23]

> Such a reordering of the world to express the capacities and reason of man was the vision behind the Renaissance humanism ... Man no longer believes there is any instinctual realm excluded from this recreated world to which he must still submit ... He believes that nature can be transformed to express the full rationality of man's own mind and to allow man to attain, within nature, all of his own purposes ... Man's own nature can be transformed, ... he can modify his own desires ... One of the things reconstructed by man in the modern period is his own sexual feelings and behavior.[24]

Man becomes *self-conscious*. Before this, man did not realize that personal relationships were different from the relationships between persons and things. But now, being newly aware of his own insides, he is able to experience another person from the other's point of view. Through personal talking with another, persons learn from experience what an "intimate" relation is. Only as two people enter each other's private, internal world, through personal conversation, can they know one another *from inside out*. The desire for this intimate relationship, and the feeling that it is the highest form of love, arises only in the modern world. "Self-consciousness contains within itself the new image of man as a being who can unify within himself the voluntary and the instinctual, the sexual and the sublime."[25] The great idea is that sex and love can be combined! To summarize this fourth historical period, which actually includes our own: self-consciousness requires the transformation of sex which is learned in adolescent petting.

Let us see how Richardson manages to put adolescent petting as we know it today in the same category with the all-male group in the Old Testament period, and monasticism in the first twelve centuries

A.D. He believes that in the first historic period sex was *naturalized,* in the second it was *segmentalized,* in the third it was *renounced,* and now for the first time in history it is able to be *transformed;* meaning that it is possible to use sexual intercourse as a means of moral communication. The old idea that "love and sex do not mix" is reversed and satisfying sex is now assumed to exist only when it is integrated with personal love.

> American sexual education aims at this personal-sexual integration, just as the patriarchal sexual education aimed at overcoming male anxiety before the power of the female, and just as early Christian . . . education aimed at the renunciation of all instinctual behavior. To educate persons for this modern integrated behavior, an "age of adolescence" had to be created. This "age of adolescence" institutionalizes a learning process of increasing sexual intimacy (by the method of "line-drawing") . . .[26]
>
> Dating, including that long process of increasing sexual intimacy sometimes called "petting" [or to be more current "making out"] is a highly stylized institution. By means of mutual experimentation between adolescent males and females possessing relatively equal degrees of inexperience, a gradual increase in sexual knowledge, self-knowledge, and intimate knowledge of others is attained so that the primordial anxiety associated with sexual intercourse is overcome.[27]
>
> To be physically intimate, but to observe strictly the line dividing the permissible from the yet unknown, is the essence of adolescent sexual morality in American society. The issue is not whether one should be sexually intimate, but how far one should go. As each unit of experience is mastered and integrated into the personal relation, enlarging the "social self," another still more intimate sexual unit is opened for exploration. During the years of adolescence the "line" is redrawn again and again in order to allow — rather to encourage — an ever-increasing experiment in intimacy . . . "line-drawing" [is used] in order to hold the expression of sexual feeling within the limit susceptible to rational voluntary control. This means that [the American petting process] places a high valuation on both virginity and on physical intimacy.[28]

So we have seen, at some length, one man's understanding of the evolution of human sexuality. It is the story of human beings trying to reconstruct their sexual behavior in order to express their ever-more complex sense of self. With the final development of abstractive intelligence, man is capable of making a distinction, or drawing a line, in the intellectual and moral order even where one cannot be seen in the physical world. Some modern moralists have condemned the "technical virgin" who in the petting process does everything *but* have intercourse.

> It may not seem, from the physical point of view, that a girl who pets to orgasm still remains a virgin. But such a distinction does make sense in the intellectual and moral order. It is a way man has of imposing his own meanings upon the physical world and integrating his instinctual and voluntary behavior.[29]

> ... In both the sexual and the intellectual orders what is at stake is the ability to expose oneself to a problematic reality, to endure the tension of contrary feelings and questions, while bearing the anxiety that such openness involves — resisting the urge toward closure.[30]

In this way we can understand that there is a correlation between the length of formal education and the length of time virginity has been maintained.

> The longer virginity is maintained [while petting is practiced], the more time adolescents have to learn the multiple discriminations required to attain to full personal-sexual intimacy. To learn these discriminations requires the development of abstractive intelligence, the ability to think of oneself as a rational and free being ... The psychological competences that undergird such a growth in sexual behavior are precisely the same competences used to do successful work in relatively abstract fields of study in a university ... The capacity to maintain virginity is, therefore, an important element in the attainment of the kind of maturity related to romantic-personal marriage and democratic society.[31]

So, if you buy this long and complicated reasoning, "making out," "petting," "necking," (or whatever the most current slang term is at the moment) is an important and good thing in contemporary psychosexual development. And if petting is important as a learning experience, virginity is even more important. Virginity is the basis for the petting process. *Not* to draw the line is to change the whole thing into foreplay, and that for the adolescent means to give up the creative tension of petting and jump into intercourse without having learned or earned enough sexual maturity to be there. Sidney Callahan has put it well:

> Man's humanity depends upon his ability to say "no"; to inhibit behavior and discriminate between different behaviors is human. The pause between thought and deed is the pause that refreshes us into humanity.[32]

The case for adolescent virginity can be argued another way also: The adolescent can be asked to sincerely try to be truthful with him/herself about the meanings of intercourse in a situation where the ultimate commitment is not being made. Sexual actions always "say" a lot more than we realize. They are always combined with powerful motives and feelings that do not have much to do with sex or innocent pleasure. Here are a few:

Sex and rebellion. Intercourse between unmarried teen-agers is often a way of expressing rebellion against authority figures.

Sex and peer pressures. It can be done because "everybody is doing it." It is the "in" thing.

Sex and quick intimacy. It can be an easy way to avoid developing other kinds of personal closeness which may take a lot of time and effort.

Sex and ego. It can be a way of proving masculinity or femininity (seeing if your plumbing really works).

Sex and seduction. It can be a way of determining how sexually powerful or seductive you are.

Sex and possessiveness. It can be a way of keeping a relationship going if you are afraid of losing him/her.

Sex and routine. It can seem to be the last and logical stage in a relationship, almost as if you are following a ritual.

Sex and barter. It can be a bargaining device (I will give you sex if you will give me something else).

Sex and illness. It can be due to a powerful psychological need because of an emotional problem (the Don Juan and the nymphomaniac).

So sexual intercourse is never just sex. It may be for animals, but for humans it always carries a lot of freight with it. None of the above "motives" can be called loving. For adolescents, it is almost impossible for a few of these motives not to be involved. Virginity for an adolescent can be an heroic choice to be emotionally honest and loving.

6
Homosexuality

Most of us are confused about homosexuality. Some homosexuals are not. They are sure it is a great way to be. Some heterosexuals are not confused. They are sure homosexuality is perverted and evil. A few years ago the press was full of the battle between representatives of these convinced groups: the Gay Liberationists and Anita Bryant. The rest of us sat back and watched the struggle. We did not learn much from it, but sometimes we were entertained. There were clever people on both sides. One letter to the editor in *Time* said, "Frankly, I believe that if my son is not safe in a classroom with a male homosexual teacher, then surely my daughter is not safe with a male heterosexual teacher."[1] Humor is a helpful release from one of the most difficult dilemmas of modern society. It elicits very strong feelings in almost everyone, because we are dealing here with some deeply rooted prejudices as well as complex and mysterious realities which are seldom understood by the average person. The experts also disagree, so nothing is simple about this subject.

Almost everyone accepts diversity and pluralism of life styles as a fact of our age. It is O.K. to be different politically, racially, religiously, but does our liberalism include a third form of being sexual on an equal basis with the "normal" two? Most homosexuals would say, "No, it does not. We are a persecuted minority and yet our life style is as 'normal' as any other." And that is where the battle seems to be drawn. What is homosexuality? The experts we usually look to in matters sexual are the psychiatrists. They are not agreed. In 1974, they officially said (the result of a majority vote, about sixty percent) in the American Psychiatric Association that homosexuality was not considered a sign of any sort of mental illness. This seems to imply for the rest of us that it is a "normal" condition. As one dissenting voter in that organization said later, "If there is one thing we *do* know about human personality, it is that males are supposed to mate with females and females are supposed to mate with males." That would seem to define what is "normal." And yet human homosexuality has been around as long as recorded history. It is certainly a normal variant. The problem finally becomes a moral one, since the real difficulty is in deciding the relative "goodness" or "badness" of the homosexual life style. We could be simplistic and say that for a Christian the only single moral yardstick is love. Can not a homosexual be as loving as anyone else? Certainly. Then why is there a problem? The homosexual Christian has his work cut out for him just as the straight Christian does — to love God, receive God's love through Christ and to love his neighbor in the best way he can. This loving includes sexual activity when appropriate, within the sexual preferences that his/her psychic structure chooses. But this does not take us far enough. We must be able to determine what the specific differences are between the two sexual styles and then place moral values on these differences. This we have to do because Gays are becoming evangelistic, if not militant. They no longer feel their sexual proclivities are less healthy, wholesome, creative, fulfilling, or valid than those of the straights. They see their style as an equal alternative, and therefore are beginning to demand the right to promote it and enhance our society by making sexual options more readily available. To quote one homosexual: "You heterosexuals work hard at trying to make all children straight. Why shouldn't we homosexuals be given an equal opportunity to promote our style?" So the problem becomes one of equal rights in the market place of social values, based on a belief that the goods to be sold are of equal worth. We have to decide.

How many are there? Some five to ten percent of the world's population are homosexually inclined, drawn emotionally and physically to members of their own sex.[2] We are talking about a minimum of 8,500,000 adult homosexuals in America today.[3] That is getting near three times the size of the Episcopal Church. At the First National Conference on Religion and the Homosexual, in 1971, the Rev. Robert Wood said, "We are here because the church, historically and hysterically, has been *the* greatest anti-homosexual force in the history of Western man."[4]

There is no equivocation about homosexuality in the Bible. It is condemned. This condemnation ranges from the extreme of Leviticus (20:13) which states, "they shall be put to death," to St. Paul's opinion that homosexuals cannot be a part of the Kingdom of God (1 Corinthians 6:9) because of their "perversion" (*Jerusalem Bible,* Romans 1:27). In Biblical times, homosexual acts were thought to be free and conscious evil choices on the part of those involved. There was no understanding of the origins of homosexuality or any concept of it as a "given" sexual orientation. Since there are now reasons to believe that in many cases homosexuality is not a free and consciously chosen sexual style, it becomes difficult to retain the simple moralism of the Bible and to condemn it as a chosen evil. For many Christians today, the Biblical approach cannot help much in dealing with the complexities of this subject.

Generally, the churches are still ambivalent regarding homosexual behavior, but in recent years they have been clear in affirming homosexuals as persons of worth. In 1970, the Lutheran church in

America officially said:

> Scientific research has not been able to provide conclusive evidence regarding the causes of homosexuality. Nevertheless, homosexuality is viewed biblically as a departure from the heterosexual structure of God's creation. Persons who engage in homosexual behavior are sinners only as are all other persons — alienated from God and neighbor. However, they are often the special and undeserving victims of prejudice and discrimination in law, law enforcement, cultural mores and congregational life. In relation to this area of concern, the sexual behavior of freely consenting adults in private is not an appropriate subject for legislation or police action. It is essential to see such persons as entitled to understanding and justice in church and community.[5]

The United Methodist Church said at its 1972 General Conference:

> Homosexuals no less than heterosexuals are persons of sacred worth, who need the ministry and guidance of the church in their struggles for human development, as well as the spiritual and emotional care of a fellowhip which enables reconciling relationships with God, with others and with self. Further, we insist that all persons are entitled to have their human and civil rights ensured.[6]

When brought to a vote, this affirmative statement was amended by the following clause: "though we do not condone the practice of homosexuality and consider this practice incompatible with Christian teaching."[7]

The Unitarian Universalist Association in 1970, "Urges all peoples immediately to bring an end to all discrimination against homosexuals, homosexuality, bisexuals and bisexuality..."[8]

The Council for Christian Social Action, United Church of Christ in 1969 "... believes that the time is long overdue for our churches to be enlisted in the cause of justice and compassion for homosexual persons."[9]

The Episcopal Church passed the following at its

1976 convention:

> Resolved, that it is the sense of this General Convention that homosexual persons are children of God, who have a full and equal claim with all other persons upon the love, acceptance, and pastoral concern and care of the Church.[10]

They also recommended that the Church, in general, engage in serious study and dialogue in the area of human sexuality.

At the next convention of the Episcopal Church in 1979, the following resolution was passed dealing with the issue of the ordaining of homosexuals: "We reaffirm the traditional teaching of the Church on marriage, marital fidelity and sexual chastity as the standard of Christian sexual morality. Candidates for ordination are expected to conform to this standard. Therefore we believe it is not appropriate for this Church to ordain a practicing homosexual, or any person who is engaged in heterosexual relations outside of marriage."

An official United Presbyterian Church task force recommended in January 1978 to the national body that homosexuals be allowed to be ordained to the Presbyterian ministry. In May of that year the General Assembly offered "definitive guidance" to its presbyteries. It declared that "unrepentant homosexual practice does not accord with the requirements for ordination . . . We conclude that homosexuality is not God's wish for humanity . . . It is a result of our living in a fallen world."

A study document on Homosexuality and the Church, published by the General Assembly of the Christian Church (Disciples of Christ) in the United States and Canada — 1977, in the *General Assembly Business Docket* claimed:

> Cross cultural studies indicate that there is no demonstrable

relation between the degree of repressive sanctions against it and the incidence of homosexuality in a society. There are powerful reinforcements of heterosexual patterns in all societies, even in those that have lenient attitudes toward homosexuality. Countries that have never had repressive laws or those that have repealed them do not appear to have higher incidence. Some cultural historians believe that rates of incidence do not vary greatly among societies and historical periods. Kinsey's research spanned three generations of subjects and found no upward or downward trend. It appears that a certain percentage of persons engage in homosexual relationships and always have, and that what changes is the public awareness rather than the incidence.

What is Homosexuality?

Is it a "natural" thing that is a part of all animal life? Sexual contacts between members of the same sex are widespread among mammals. But the exact significance of such behavior varies. According to one psychiatrist,

> Popular opinion and homosexual apologists to the contrary, there is no such thing as homosexual behavior which includes climax, or even (between males) intromission, in the animal kingdom. The rare exceptions occur under the extreme circumstances of artificial stress, such as overcrowding of rats in laboratories.[11]

On the other hand, we read in one of the standard textbooks,

> ... there have been observations of anal intercourse between male macaque monkeys both in captivity and in the wild ... Two general conclusions are quite clear: First, homosexual behavior is never the dominant sexual outlet in any human or animal species. Second, references to certain kinds of behavior as "natural" and to others as "unnatural" are difficult to substantiate on the evidence of what actually occurs in nature.[12]

Freud also had difficulty deciding about how to categorize homosexuality. In a famous letter to a mother of a homosexual, he wrote,

> Homosexuality is assuredly no advantage, but it is nothing to be ashamed of, no vice, no degradation, it cannot be classified as an illness; we consider it to be a variation of the sexual function produced by a certain arrest of sexual development.[13]

And yet, Freud said over and over that the libido has only one normal and natural goal: heterosexual coitus. In the above quote we see his ambivalence. If it is a variation, then it must be one of the ways the sexual instinct normally fulfills itself. But he ascribes it to "a certain arrest in sexual development," which is not the norm. The point is, Freud did not want to label the condition "illness" because he believed a homosexual could be psychologically stable in spite of the inherent immaturity involved.[14] Dr. Ruth Barnhouse is an Episcopalian and Harvard psychiatrist. A homosexual, she said, is a person who has failed to complete his/her emotional development, and she urged acceptance of them as persons with one special trait of immaturity. "Everyone has pockets of immaturity," she said. There are others in and out of the church whose lives have been just as "flawed with immaturities and mistakes" as homosexuals. "Look at me," she demanded.

> I eloped when I was 17 and had two marriages and two divorces. That's my problem. That's the best I could do . . . Some homosexuals are living with responsible homosexual lifestyles and doing the best they can do.[15]

But while admitting the gay person deserves the same respect and understanding which other people with shortcomings receive, this is not the same as endorsing his/her lifestyle, she emphasized.

Then there are others who disagree and feel that homosexuality does not imply abnormality or immaturity. Psychologist Alan Bell of the Institute for Sex Research at Indiana University has concluded:

> The fact is, almost without exception, whenever nonclinical samples of homosexuals are compared with equivalent heterosexual samples, very few if any differences are found in their psychological functioning ... Whenever differences are found, they usually do not stand up in other studies, or ... the kinds of analyses that are done make it difficult to conclude that the differences are a function of a person's sexual orientation *per se*. Perhaps more homosexuals than heterosexuals seek professional help or have attempted suicide, but it is as easy to interpret these behaviors as the consequence of being homosexual in a society which is hostile to homosexuality as it is to conclude that homosexuality necessarily involves or is caused by psychological maladjustment...[16]

Seward Hiltner of Princeton Theological Seminary wrote:

> As to the causes of homosexuality in males, there is so far no conclusive evidence that physiological or biochemical factors are involved (but it may eventually be found that some such factors are contributory), and there is general agreement that homosexual patterns are "learned." But the complexities of the "learning" are very poorly understood.[17]

If there are grounds for believing that it is a socially acquired inclination (which is contrary to what the Christian Church — Disciples of Christ — said in its study document quoted from previously), then certainly society has some responsibilities for either fostering or discouraging those environmental factors. If this life style is in some sense a "choice" of character, as many homosexuals insist, then that choice may be influenced by various things, including the social atmosphere or sustained exposure to homosexual role models.[18] According to the theories of Harry Stack Sullivan, who was himself a homosexual, and who created the interpersonal theory of psychiatry, preadolescence is a key time in developmental process when homosexuality may develop. Then the child begins to form peer relationships in which there are equality, mutuality, and reciprocity between members. Without an intimate companion, the preadolescent becomes the victim of a desperate loneliness. During this period, the main problem is the development of a pattern of homosexual activity. The physiological changes of puberty are experienced by the youth as feelings of lust; out of these feelings the lust dynamism emerges and begins to assert itself in the personality. There is a separation of erotic need from the need for intimacy; the erotic need focuses on a member of the opposite sex, while the need for intimacy remains fixated upon a member of the same sex.

> If these two needs do not become divorced, the young person displays a homosexual rather than a heterosexual orientation. Sullivan points out that many of the conflicts of adolescence arise out of the opposing needs for sexual gratification, security, intimacy. Early adolescence persists until the person has found some stable pattern of performances which satisfies his genital drives.[19]

Irving Bieber in *Homosexuality* (1962) reported a famous study of the family pattern in which homosexuals were raised. It was characterized by a close-binding and/or seductive mother with a distant and/or absent and/or hostile father. Many experts now feel that this theory of etiology has been disproved or discarded. But no one ever claimed it was the *only* cause, or that it could be demonstrated in all cases. W. Paul Jones, of the St. Paul School of Theology in Kansas City, Missouri, wrote an article in *Pastoral Psychology*, December 1970, describing experiences with homosexuals in that city.

> The almost universal story [told by homosexuals about their own histories] disclosed the emergence of homosexual behavior as a process of self-discovery, and that the traditional transition from early adolescent homo-sexual crushes or gang loyalty to bi-sexual interest never really occurs for the

> homosexual. It was a mystery to each of us who are heterosexual when in our youth others of the same sex in our gang began to express an awkward and unpredicted preference for females. In time, the advancement to our own puberty made this "oddity" entirely understandable; but the as yet latent homosexual gains no such illumination. Increasingly, one's friends develop sexual interest in the opposite sex, until one finds himself alone, interested in male companionship which other males no longer hold in high priority. Then one day, despite one's fear, he finds something peculiar occurring in this feeling as he meets a particularly attractive male — an attraction with all the emotional overtones that others know in their first male-female crush. And so it continues to be — while others look appreciatively at female beauty, watch motion pictures with interest (all of which are heterosexual), understand advertising with sexual overtones, etc., etc. — the homosexual is alienated in all of these countless arenas of ordinary life. He fights his own feelings until he finds that he is fighting himself.[20]

One thing that is clear in all this is the fact that human beings are just beginning to understand homosexuality, either through scientific investigation or simple human empathy. We all want a society that is more sensitive to differences in sexual response. And as Irving Singer writes:

> . . . we may encourage people to find their satisfaction through any behavior that does not harm others; but we cannot enunciate general principles that would enable an individual to choose a life which is most suitable for *him*. To do that, we would need a kind of certitude about various empirical questions which no science is able to provide as yet. These are questions about innate biological and hormonal forces, psychological patterns of development, social determinants, moral consequences, and in general, the human capacity for achieving happiness through one or another sexual orientation.[21]

We do not have the knowledge or wisdom to answer questions like these as yet. So what we do about these problems will probably continue to be the product of a majority rule. Since homosexuality remains a minority interest for human beings, it will probably not be allowed to function as an equally viable means by which everyone may express his or her sexuality.

What about Christian sexual morality as it applies not to the state of being homosexual, but to its practice? Should moral standards be any different for homosexuals than for heterosexuals? According to Katchadourian and Lunde,

> Male homosexuals generally have short-term relationships, though some ties may be very intense... Jealousy is notorious. It is said to be more common among male than female homosexuals. Some homosexuals ascribe it to their being in a closed and persecuted community and anticipate that it will be less prevalent as attitudes toward homosexuals change.[22]

A college chaplain in Tennessee has made it well known among the Gay community that he would be willing to perform a marriage between homosexuals if they would promise that it would last for five years. He has never had anyone take him up on it. Norman Pittenger, a leading Anglican theologian, has written:

> If they [homosexuals] are to know human love at all, it must be in this way, and if they are to express that love at all, it must be in this way. Control is needed, of course, as it is with heterosexuals. But to insist on the homosexual's absolute denial of all physical expression is to ask him to become, in spite of himself, a celibate — a state for which he may have no calling and in which he finds himself in danger of killing what he believes to be deepest and best in his life; namely, his urge to love another and to act on that urge. I have mentioned the need for "control," and by that I mean such a mastering of self as shall move the homosexual toward intimate relationships with someone to whom he can give himself in mutuality, faithfulness, sharing, and as much permanence as the two can manage. This is not easy, nor has society made it a simple matter. One can understand why many homosexuals, unable or unwilling to establish a relationship which is intentionally loyal, faithful and permanent, are driven to promiscuity and "one-night stands." To be sure, so also with heterosexuals, though *they* have the backing of society in their effort to

establish such a relationship, whereas the homosexual usually does not ... I believe the day is coming, is almost here, when the homosexual male or female will be seen as simply a human being like everybody else — a person created in God's image, on the way to becoming a created lover, in defection from the goal but helped to move toward it through the healthy use of the particular homosexual drive rather than through its utter denial.[23]

Pittenger recommends that these relationships be with "as much permanence as the two can manage." That sounds as if a lower standard is to be applied to them than the life-long monogamous demand that is the meaning behind the vows made in heterosexual marriages. Maybe if one truly understands how powerful the pressures are against homosexuality from society as it is (and we are all responsible for that), then all you can humanly ask is "do the best you can to stay together." But then, if that becomes the limit of the commitment demanded by the church, is not the church in effect saying homosexual marriage is quite a different thing from heterosexual marriage? In the latter, the *vow* is of the utmost *help*. It helps to say, in effect,

I know this is going to be difficult. At times all my emotions will say "get out," but for two reasons I promise that under those conditions I will act on this willed commitment, not my feelings: 1. It gives you (my mate) the security and freedom which I want you to have in my love. You don't have to earn it. You can simply count on it being there. 2. It helps me realize that a large part of marriage is having problems and using them creatively. Interpersonal problem solving is of the essence of marriage, not a sign that it should be terminated.[24]

How does the church decide *not* to give the kind of help that requiring a vow bestows? Let us avoid this difficult question for now and say that the church should, theoretically, demand the vow of permanence in all marriages. Are there any other problems involved in homosexual marriages big enough to eliminate the whole idea?

Professor Jones would say no. He tells an interesting story:

> On a Sunday evening in the summer of 1968, there was a wedding scheduled for a Methodist church in Kansas City, Missouri. At first glance this was nothing seemingly extraordinary, other than the fact, perhaps, that the service was to be a double marriage, before two Methodist clergymen. But the radical nature of this event is clear, for the newly written liturgy called for the two women to make covenant vows unto death to one another, and the two men were to bear identical witness. The marriage service was to be the blessing of the church, perhaps for the first time, of a homosexual and of a lesbian marriage. This event had its beginning when the two ministers, who had practiced for some time in the local young adult night ministry and in the formation of a homosexual organization . . . received a letter written jointly by two lesbians. In words of undeniable beauty, the situation was simply stated. Each of the women (in their thirties) had a child from a previous marriage . . . Gradually, each woman came to discover that she was lesbian. It was during this time that the two met and were deeply drawn to each other. In the relation they found together that which each had been deprived throughout life (both had known tragic childhood rejection). Frightened by their discovery of deep personal attachment, they imposed a six-month total separation, with no communication permitted. The time lapse, however, only intensified the relationship. They rented a house (both having responsible jobs) and endeavored to create a stable family life for their children and themselves. The conclusion they drew was that their "feelings" had long since grown into a willed covenant for life, and intention to be "one flesh." Their request to the ministers was frightfully simple: could these ministers make possible a context in which these women might make this life-pledge publicly before God? . . . is the homosexual excluded by definition from entry into this central arena of humanness? . . . It would seem to follow that sexual abstinence . . . is no moral answer but a fundamental deprivation which cuts at essential humanness . . . Therefore we conclude that, given the constitutional limits defining the homosexual, profound relation between two members of the same sex *is not only morally permissible but is to be sought, encouraged, supported, and enabled with all the powers at our command.* There is no substitute for such relation, and of it the homosexual must not be denied. And this relation includes at its very core the sexual experience uninhibited by any thought

> of techniques of "sexual normality" . . . And . . . with homosexual marriage must go every effort to provide a supporting framework: increasing civil rights, a homosexual social center as hub of an authentic subculture, a means of communication and outreach . . . community support for marriages — and at the foundation of all this should be the church, for she above all can provide the moral legitimacy and confirmation without which self-acceptance is so tentative.[25]

The double marriage never took place in a church. No minister dared to make his church available. That was nine years ago and maybe things have changed by now. At least the churches are talking about the problem.

George F. Will, writing in Newsweek, takes a different view:

> If ratified, the Equal Rights Amendment might easily be construed to invalidate laws prohibiting homosexual marriages. Homosexuals complain that such laws constitute discrimination that denies them tax, social security and inheritance advantages, "family" health insurance, and other benefits. Next will come the right of homosexuals to adopt children, to have homosexuality "fairly represented" as an "alternative lifestyle" in every child's sex-education classes, and in literature in public libraries. If you think that this is a caricature of possibilities, consider the case of the Minneapolis man who applied to be a Big Brothers companion to a fatherless boy. He listed as a reference a renowned homosexual who had "married" his male roommate in college, so officials asked the applicant if he was a homosexual. He said his "serious affections" were for males, so the officials said they would tell any mother before he could be Big Brother to her son. He cried "discrimination!" and the city civil rights officials suggested Big Brothers should stop inquiring about "sexual preferences"; that Big Brothers staffers should attend seminars given by homosexuals, and suggested that Big Brothers should undertake "affirmative action" by advertising for volunteers in homosexual periodicals.[26]*

Dr. Barnhouse is also opposed to homosexual marriage. She writes:

---

*Copyright 1977 by Newsweek, Inc. ALL RIGHTS RESERVED. Reprinted by permission.

> Freud correctly perceived in sex something absolutely fundamental to all other human attitudes and feelings, but he did not discern the true reason: it is in fact a holy symbol of union and reconciliation against which sacrilege is perilously easy to commit . . . This insight is preserved not only in the image of the Church as the bride of Christ, but in the institution of marriage as a sacrament. No other phenomenon of human existence can symbolize the vision of the sacramental universe, in which all things are harmoniously connected, and at the same time manifest the tragic discontinuity which man inflicted on himself and his world through the Fall . . . With respect to sexuality itself, men and women have very different ways of experiencing and expressing it. This makes the ancient prescription "they two shall become one flesh" still more mysterious. What is involved is a decisive and ongoing encounter with "otherness," a reconciliation of opposites, and this is what gives sex its potentially sacramental character . . . Such a view entirely rules out the possibility of the solemnization of "homosexual marriages," something which is being proposed in some quarters. The sacrament of marriage is not to be diminished to the level of community affirmation that "you're OK." It has meanings, most of which we have only begun to tap, which have roots deep in the mystery of the sexual union of man and woman and with these we must not tamper.[27]

Having presented all these widely divergent views, I must at this point use an old cliché: If the reader is not confused he does not understand the problem.

In concluding this chapter, it might be well to remind ourselves that anyone's sexual identity tells us only about a small part of that person. We are all much more than our sexual preferences. *No* definition of a human being even begins to describe him/her. The full truth about any one of us is always complex, hidden and yet to be revealed.

In summary, we must remind ourselves of the great ignorance about every aspect of this subject with which we are all afflicted. We're just beginning to learn. However, the overarching principle of procreation, as at least a possibility, would seem to imply that homosexuality is an abnormality in human behavior. Also, as we have said previously, our sex organs themselves point to the natural need for completion by the appropriate organ of the opposite sex. Therefore, all things being equal, a heterosexual approach to life is likely to be more rewarding. BUT, and this is a big but, all things are seldom equal. Each individual has his own unique set of assets and liabilities, and we all must try to be the best person we can, given the gifts we have to work with and God's grace which we continually need.

We said at the beginning that this was a very emotional issue. Your feelings have probably been shoved around considerably while you were reading. One helpful thing to do would be to take a while to look at those feelings. Why do you think you feel the way you do about the subject of homosexuality? The answers you come up with will probably be more helpful than any of the intellectualizing that this chapter has demanded. So, if the chapter has mainly gotten you upset (which I imagine will be the comments of most readers), do not feel too negative. That can be the beginning of some positive insights.

7
Marriage

Marriage is still the basic social structure for most of us. There are about forty-two million families in the United States right now with husband and wife living together. Marriage is everywhere. However, there has recently arisen around all these marriages a social atmosphere that questions the value of traditional monogamy. Is it really the best way to live? Is it not too confining for personal growth? No one in our society can avoid hearing these questions, and as a result there is much doubt and uncertainty about marriage as we now know it. There are many different answers being given, and many people are already living out their theories of how marriage should be improved. This chapter is divided into two parts. The first is a non-judgmental look at what some people are saying and doing to change marriage. The second is a reassessment of traditional life-long monogamy.

Some Quotes from the Marriage Critics

The O'Neills' book, *Open Marriage*, is the most successful book of its kind. Since writing it Nena O'Neill has written another book expressing a much more conservative view.[1] But it is the first book that has been the most influential (it sold about three and one-half million copies). At the time of writing *Open Marriage*, they believed strongly that marriage must "open up."

> It should be understood that man (and we mean both sexes) is not sexually monogamous by nature, evolution or force of habit. In all societies around the world in which he has been

enjoined to become sexually monogamous in marriage . . . he has failed to live up to that standard . . . always he fails, in numbers large enough to make that failure significant . . . That leads us to an inevitable question: is it the "unfaithful" human being who is the failure, or is it the standard itself? . . . monogamy as a standard . . . gives rise to some extremely unpleasant side effects . . . It implies ownership, demands sexual exclusivity, and denies both equality and identity. It perverts jealousy into a "good . . . [it] is supposed to show you "care."[2]

In *Beyond Monogamy,* the editors write,

. . . we have selected the term "transmarital to convey a generally positive or at least sympathetic meaning to . . . any sexual activity, interaction, relationship, or ideological scheme which aids and abets the transformation of the institutional superstructure and/or the interpersonal infrastructure of traditional marriage in a way which allows greater relative interpersonal autonomy and independence and fosters a greater capacity for intimacy and sociability. It includes . . . 1. Married persons who engage in direct and indirect sexual activities with a person other than their primary partner, but with the knowledge and consent of their partner . . . 2. Couples who cohabit on a regular basis and who have established an ongoing relationship . . . [without] legal and/or religious certification. 3. Group marriages, communal living groups . . .[3]

The consequences for marriage are significant and dramatic. By eliminating or at least reducing the deceit associated with conventional adulterous behavior and by transcending the intramarital demands of sexual exclusivity, and at the same time achieving new levels of candor and freedom about sexuality, the conjugal relationship can be transformed into something very different which may be more trying and challenging but also more rewarding and fulfilling . . . From this perspective, those couples [who cannot be transmaritally active] . . . can be viewed as suffering from a condition of insecurity and dyadic pathos, which may well become . . . pathogenic . . . they can be seen as suffering from what might be called an adultery-evasion complex or trust-deficiency syndrome, obscure names for altogether common maladies.[4]

Ronald Mazur, in his book *The New Intimacy,* says.

> Traditional monogamy ... no longer provides for mutual self-realization. We consider traditional monogamy, with its rigid requirement for exclusive devotion and affection, even though hallowed by the theological concept of fidelity, to be a culturally approved mass neurosis.[5]
>
> For too long, traditional moralists have been passively allowed to pre-empt other conscientious life-styles by propagating the unproven assumptions that we cannot love more than one person (of the opposite sex) concurrently; that co-marital or extramarital sex always destroys marriage.[6]

James R. Smith adds from *Beyond Monogamy,*

> From an interpersonal point of view, living in a monogamous relationship is not unlike having sex with one's clothing on: it diminishes sensitivity and restricts movement. From a radical perspective, strict monogamy is seen as fetishistic, for it makes a sexual fetish (not to mention a virtual possession) of one person exclusively.[7]

Mazur goes on to say:

> Persons participating in an open-ended marriage covenant not only with each other, but with the Family of Man. In a profound sense all children are their children, and all adults are their loved ones. Within such marriages the possibility of adultery is totally absent because exclusion, possessiveness, and jealousy have no place in the relationship ... [It is possible] to create a model of marriage — a covenant — monogamous in the sense that it is based upon an intended lifetime commitment between two, but which nevertheless is open-ended because it does not exclude the freedom to have any number of intimate relationships with others.[8]
>
> What a new model of open-ended marriage seeks to promote is risk-taking in trust; the warmth of loving without anxiety; the extension of affection; the excitement and pleasure of knowing sensuously a variety of other persons; the enrichment which personalities can contribute to each other; the joy of being fully alive in every encounter.[9]

The Alternatives to Marriage

Open Marriage

[This] . . . can be defined as a relationship in which the partners are committed to their own and to each other's growth. It is an honest and open relationship of intimacy and self-disclosure based on the equal freedom and identity of both partners. Supportive caring and increasing security in individual identities make possible the sharing of self-growth with a meaningful other who encourages and anticipates his own and his mate's growth. It is a relationship that is flexible enough to allow for change and that is constantly being renegotiated in the light of changing needs . . . The guidelines are: living for now, realistic expectations, privacy, role flexibility, open and honest communication, open companionship [relating to others, including the opposite sex, outside the primary unit of husband and wife, as an auxiliary avenue for growth], equality, identity, and trust.[10]

The expectations of closed marriage — the major one being that one partner will be able to fulfill all of the other's needs (emotional, social, sexual, economic, intellectual, and otherwise) — present obstacles to growth and attitudes that foster conflict between partners.[11]

Fidelity is redefined in *Open Marriage*.

Sexual fidelity is the false god of closed marriage, a god to whom partners submit (or whom they defy) for all the wrong reasons and often at the cost of the very relationship which that god is supposed to protect . . . Fidelity in the closed marriage is the measure of *limited* love, *diminished* growth and *conditional* trust. This fixation in the end defeats its own purpose, encouraging deception, sowing the seeds of mistrust and limiting the growth of both partners and so of the love between them. Fidelity, in its root meaning denotes allegiance and fealty to a duty or obligation. But love and sex should never be seen in terms of duty or obligation, as they are in closed marriage. They should be seen as experiences to be shared and enjoyed together, as they are in open marriage. Fidelity then is redefined in open marriage, as commitment to your own growth, equal commitment to your partner's growth, and a sharing of the self-discovery accomplished through such growth. It is loyalty and faithfulness to growth, to integrity of self and respect for the other, not to a sexual and psychological bondage to each other.[12]

Adultery

In an essay by a group of English Friends called *Towards a Quaker View of Sex* (1963) the idea is maintained that possibly adultery can be constructive.

> We recognize that while most examples of the "eternal triangle" are produced by boredom and primitive misconduct, others may arise from the fact that the very experience of loving one person with depth and perception may sensitize a man or woman to the lovable qualities in others ... The man who swallows the words "I love you" when he meets another woman, may in that moment and for that reason begin to resent his wife's existence.[13]

In *Honest Sex:*

> We find that sexual relations with persons other than a spouse are becoming more common. When other criteria of appropriateness are fulfilled, such relations do not necessarily destroy or hurt a marriage, nor do they inflict an unbearable hurt on the partner not involved. Indeed, when human need is paramount, such relationships can serve as the vehicle of faithfulness to God.[14]

> The Christian way is one of a kind of abandoned self-giving ... It is utterly ridiculous to say on the one hand, "Greater love hath no man than this, that he lay down his life for his friends," and to assert immediately that it is impossible and unnatural for a man (or woman) to agree to share his (or her) spouse with another.[15]

> What of two young couples, neighbors and close friends, when one husband is away in the Army for one or two years, where the husband left behind is playing the father role for the neighbor's children, helping the wife with her car, her income tax form, her leaky basement? Is it right only to help with the physical needs but not her needs for companionship, friendship, love?[16]

> When deep relationships exist between the persons, we find the danger from such experience not to be prohibitive if the spouse is progressively informed of the development of the relationship and the marriage itself is secure ... It is important not to ask the wrong question nor use the wrong words. It is

important not to ask whether coitus has occurred; it is important to avoid words such as adultery. The important question is: Were relations deepened so as to make all the persons concerned more able to become whole, to give to others and so on?[17]

Masters and Johnson call extramarital sex something that is the result of a fundamental human paradox.

A person feels most fully alive when he can be stimulated by the challenge of the unknown and yet have the security of the known to give him the confidence he needs to try something different than he has attempted in the past. The pleasure of being alive depends to a considerable degree on an individual's ability to include both elements in his life ... For many people ... a monogamous marriage means putting an end to this alternation between the new and the old ... at least as far as sex is concerned ... But the wish that it could be otherwise remains strong ... They half want to be persuaded that having one married partner need not mean having just one sexual partner, that any modern couple should be able to enjoy the challenge of extramarital affairs and still maintain the security of their marriage. Looked at one way, it amounts to offering husbands and wives the opportunity to have their cake and eat it, too. Looked at another way, it amounts to a magic cure for marital doldrums. Either way, the lure is powerful.[18]

O.S. English writes:

If [1977] years of monogamy have not brought people of the world above the level of alcoholism, drug-taking, bribery, crime, rioting war, and insanity, any gain, which might lie in an affair ... seems worth full discussion at least. The affair has not been devoid of heartaches, pain, and discord, but neither is any other human activity, even tennis, pinochle, skiing, or horticulture. Adultery is being practiced by large numbers of devotees. Why not permit its reality and thereby give it an opportunity to succeed or fail within more public scrutiny and a more open knowledge of whether its results and effects are so very good or so very bad![19]

Contract Cohabitation

Contract Cohabitation is an eating, sleeping, and liv-

ing arrangement between employer and employee, based on written or unwritten employment contract. This obviously means that it is an unequal relationship from the beginning. Sex is allowed, but can not be demanded or restrained; both parties are free to be together, apart, or with someone else. It has been tried and written about in a book by that name by Edmund L. Van Duesen. It is not a theoretical approach to marriage. It is one man's personal experience and therefore is a description of one experiment. He feels it has given him his first chance to be in a close, cherishing relationship, yet be completely himself, without any of the concessions and compromises that characterize marriage. Personal freedom is one of the great values he sees in an arrangement that simply transfers from office to home, all the laws and customs that govern our working environment. Mr. Van Deusen tried orthodox marriage, "living with someone," and living alone, and finally worked out this alternative. He writes,

> It wasn't so much that I wanted to be free of any relationship. I just wanted, once in my life, to be a real "me," to discover the hard edges of my own personality — not the diffused, intermingled personality of two people, living together or married . . . my wife and I had grown so together that it was impossible to tell where I ended and she began.[20]

One thing he found out about himself very quickly was that for him there is a difference between "sex" and "bed." He said it was like the difference between food and water.

> I can go for a while without sex, but not without bed . . . So I'm a bed addict, incurably hooked. I need to be held, just like a baby . . . it really doesn't make too much difference who the bed partner is . . . It's the holding that counts, not the identity of the person.[21]

Sex is not a part of the contract. As he explains:

> Neither is laughter, watching sunsets, holding hands, or any other mutual pleasure. They can be neither demanded nor restrained. We're free to be together, or not together... Sex is a natural instinct, so its natural state is good. You have to work at it to make it bad. If sex is bad, it means that something else is wrong somewhere.[22]

> [When] I was taking the first essential step toward Contract Cohabitation, I was struggling to be honest with myself, to accept the fact that all of us, in the final analysis, march to our own selfish drum — that we get into trouble when we try to syncopate the beat with the rhythm of another person's drum.[23]

> All of our cultural training is to "think of the other person first." But the special value to Contract Cohabitation is that it allows two persons to live in close companionship, yet selfishly retain their own identities.[24]

The pay is entirely in cash, not in emotions. The label "employee" is seen as better than "wife" in terms of financial benefits and personal independence.

Serial Monogamy (Divorce)

Most people with serious marital difficulties do not try any of the more esoteric options as a way out. They take the one with legal acceptability: Divorce. Each year this approach to marital problem solving becomes easier, more acceptable and more popular. Between 1639 and 1692 only 42 couples in the entire Massachusetts Colony were divorced — not even one a year. Two centuries later, 700 divorces were granted in Victorian England in one year. It was scandalous. In America in the same year, 1886, there were 25,000 divorces. In 1920 it was one divorce for every seven American marriages. In 1940 it was one for every six; in 1960 one for every four; in 1972 one for every three. In 1976, according to the statistics of the U.S. Department of Health, Education and Welfare, there were five divorces for every ten marriages.[25] In California in 1973, there were two divorces for every three marriages. As no-fault divorce laws become more popular around the country, the other states may well catch up with California.[26] It is an almost unbelievable progression of statistics, is it not? It may well be one of the most significant changes ever to take place in human history. It almost seems that a large part of our society treats first marriages as if they were trial runs. Like a growing-up period for grownups.[27]

Group Sex

"Swinging" is another term for this type of permissive sexual behavior. It is based on the following convictions: Sexual intercourse, like verbal intercourse, should in no way be limited by the fact that a couple is married or living together. All sexual relationships must be acknowledged; no secrecy or deception. Sexual pleasure is to be taken whenever, wherever, and however it is found — as a game in which any number can play.[28] Sex is looked on pretty much as other people think of tennis, as fun. According to Smith and Smith:

> If swingers indulge in their activities solely from sexual boredom, . . . then it would seem that sexual play and sexual variety, pursued in a sensitive, mature, and integrated manner, might be a perfect tonic, so long as the tonic is not also toxic, a fact that must be . . . determined . . . on the normative maxim — fun is a good thing as long as it spoils nothing better.[29]

One swinger described it this way:

> . . . in the beginning we found it was a stimulating thought and a stimulating thing to act on; and bringing more people into both of our sex lives eliminated the conflicts of jealousy and the insecurities of each of us going outside our marriage separately. We were doing something together that was enhancing our own sexual relationship.[30]

Another has been quoted as saying:

> ... there is a difference between swinging with people with whom you've developed a relationship and swinging for fun on a spontaneous basis with a very large group of people you don't know and can't get terribly close to because there isn't very much time. It isn't erosive of your closer relationships, and to do it with a large group can be just a grand amount of fun. I think *fun* expresses it ...[31]

One wife said:

> I think our approach was quite a bit different. Sleeping with other people is very much integrated into our lives. I personally got into it because I didn't think marriage meant sexual exclusivity. I felt I was a person, and there were all kinds of other people I could get to know, and I knew that having sex with them wouldn't harm our marriage. That went for both of us. But people we're excited about are in our lives anyway, they're not strangers. For instance, Gary is sleeping with the wife of the head of his department and his secretary and one of his students, and you know, it's completely integrated into our lives, and we've never sought people just for sex; we even avoid that.[32]

Casual Sex

This activity is the one-night or weekend sexual encounter with a stranger or strangers. Ronald Mazur, in *The New Intimacy*, believes this can be a good thing:

> Should this be any less enjoyable or satisfying because there hasn't been time for the development of communication and mutual appreciation? ... "Casual" sex with a stranger can be unpleasant, humiliating, and even dangerous (e.g., VD or emotionally unstable behavior). But it can be a positive experience for people who know themselves fairly well, who are perceptive in evaluating the personality and intentions of others, and who explore mutual expectations verbally (even if briefly). It seems as if there are ever-increasing numbers of people who are being sensitized to tenderness, caring, and understanding; people who also have few sexual hangups and a strong need for physical, sensual closeness. Such people can often recognize each other within minutes. When the "vibes"

are right, further nonverbal explorations take place. The "casual" relationship can be quite heavy. And it can be a memorable and liberating experience.[33]

In Defense of Traditional Monogamy

In the six "alternatives to marriage" just described, we can see so powerfully the frantic efforts of people to resolve the great dilemma of marriage: Men and women naturally want to possess each other completely; men and women naturally want to be free of each other. Therefore, two great fears alternate in marriage, the one of loneliness and the other of bondage. Every new "arrangement" between the sexes is an attempt to satisfy one or the other of these impulses and to some degree avoid the creative tension between the two which is the essence of traditional monogamy. To be in a monogamous marriage is to be both bound and free at the same time. This is not a strange thing for Christians, since all of theology is a context for it.

> There is a fundamental distinction in the Godhead itself between Father, Son and Holy Spirit, and yet an indissoluble bond between them; a radical distinction between Creator and creature, and yet a covenant links them. Derivatively, there is a distinction between soul and body, but a self unites them; sexuality distinguishes man and woman, but the covenant of marriage binds them.[34]

To be totally one with someone else is also to become more and more your own unique self. The miracle in marriage which can accomplish this amazing reconciliation of opposites is the covenant of love. To love is to bind the self, to give, to unite. And yet it is not an elimination of freedom; it is the fulfillment of freedom. We are free in order to choose where we will bind, and give and unite. And in doing just that — in loving — we fulfill ourselves and experience within ourselves a new depth of freedom. Marriage is really the last and closest in a long line of similar miracles: God is one, and yet when Christians realized that he was also three, God became more real; God and man are one in Christ, and yet in Christ, God is more "for us" than he has ever been; and so humans are ennobled. In marriage, man and woman are one, and yet in marriage, each becomes more masculine and more feminine.

Indissolubility

"Pleasure" and "fun" are often cited as the reason for and the result of the alternate styles of marriage. I think a better word to use in connection with traditional marriage is "joy." This is a more complex word for a much more complicated value. Joy in marriage is known through our readiness to enter into the responsibilities it brings. All joy grows out of responsiveness and responsibility. In struggling to relate in this way to one other person, you also find youself able to respond more fully to the pathos and loveliness of the whole of humankind. This is what the indissolubility of marriage is all about. It means, "This is your partner, *through* him/her you may discover the whole of mankind. If you want to by-pass him/her because you want more, you will discover that you get less."[35] The relationship of marriage becomes your unique window into the depths of all other human lives. Therefore, it can no more be destroyed than the other relationships which arise out of marriage; e.g., father and son, brother and sister, etc. The promise of marriage lies in being for the spouse's best welfare no matter what. It is the promise of willed love for now and the future.

But indissolubility does not only mean that you believe the future will be the context for more love. It also means you believe in the past of this love. How common it is for one spouse to say or think, "Why did I ever marry him/her!" At times of tension, that choice of partner made years ago may seem to have been one of the great mistakes of one's life. It is to a great extent true that your choice of a lifelong marriage partner was the most irrational choice you ever made. This does not mean it was a careless, haphazard decision. It merely means your unconscious mind had more to do with making the decision than your conscious mind. Indissolubility means, among other things, I trust what my unconscious mind did back then.

The struggle to find a mate starts very early indeed. The preschooler in those early years decides the choice is going to be his/her opposite sex parent. But that desire is permanently thwarted by the presence of that great rival, the other parent. This first unsuccessful choice conditions us very powerfully, and it becomes part of our unconscious. When we eventually choose our "second" and final love, that choice is greatly influenced by the determination of the unconscious mind to redress that old defeat by winning it this time. And the way it wins is to make the choice based on some of the same factors involved the first time.

With the conscious mind, one cannot know a person well enough to make the ultimate decision about him/her. That is why the old adage is so true, "You always marry a stranger." And yet, we can depend greatly on what the unconscious mind is doing in all this. If we are as rational about this choice as we can be, meaning: wait until you are mature before trying to make it; give yourself enough time in making the decision; consult with others about how they see the relationship; use professional counseling; pray about it, *then*, having been rational, we can trust in our unconscious to take care of the rest and make a good choice.

It is later, during the inevitable battles that take

place whenever two people try to intermesh their personalities, that this faith in the past is very important. The struggles with one's spouse, the demands that are made to change and grow, no matter how much we want to avoid them, can be believed to be exactly the ones needed. This is so because they were handpicked by the unconscious that wisely knew what kind of person was needed to give exactly the kind of problems that would best lead to fulfillment and growth. Indissolubility means "I trust the past of our relationship as well as the future."

Normally, indissolubility means sticking with marriage under all circumstances. But because it is the promise of love, there can arise situations in which because of love (the same reason you normally would stay in the relationship), you decide to end it. When divorce is the most loving thing to do (not the easiest or the most gracious), it is an occasion in which love is best served by not continuing to love in the bond of matrimony. In such a situation, divorce is the true expression of the commitment of marriage, which was to love under all circumstances.

Freedom

George Gilder does not think sex is free. He starts out his book, *Sexual Suicide*, this way:

> It is time to declare that sex is too important a subject to leave to the myopic crowd of happy hookers, Dr. Feelgoods, black panthers, white rats, answer men, evangelical lesbians, sensuous psychiatrists, retired baseball players, pornographers, dolphins, swinging priests, displaced revolutionaries, polymorphous perverts, and Playboy philosophers — all bouncing around on waterbeds and typewriters and television talk shows, making "freedom" ring the cash registers of the revolution. Nothing is free, least of all sex . . . [36]

Mr. Gilder has written another very realistic article:

In Defense of Monogamy. He elaborates (and I quote him at length) his reasons for believing that free sex in our society could well eliminate some vital freedoms. He feels strongly that to remove restrictions on sexual activity is not to bring equality and community.

> It brings ever more vicious sexual competition. The women become "easier" for the powerful to get — but harder for others to keep. Divorces become "easier" — but remarriage is extremely difficult for abandoned older women. Marriages become more "open" — open not only for the partners to get out but also for the powerful to get in.[37]
>
> Monogamy is central to any democratic social contract designed to prevent a breakdown of society into "war of every man against every other man." In order to preserve order, a man may relinquish liberty, prosperity, and power to the state. But if he has to give up his wife to his boss, he is no longer a man. A society of open sexual competition, in which the rich and powerful — or even the sexually attractive — can command large numbers of women is a society with the most intolerable hierarchy of all . . . Monogamy is egalitarianism in the realm of love. It is a mode of rationing. It means — to put it crudely — one to a customer. Competition is intense enough even so, because of the sexual inequality of human beings. But under a regime of monogamy there are limits. One may covet one's neighbor's wife, one may harbor fantasies of teeny boppers, but one generally leaves it at that. One does not leave one's wife when she grows older, to take a woman who would otherwise go to a younger man. Thus a balance is maintained and each generation gets its only true sexual rights: the right to a wife or husband and the right to participate in the future of the race through children . . .[38]
>
> Monogamy is designed to minimize the effect of . . . inequalities — to prevent the powerful of either sex from disrupting the familial order. In practice, however, the chief offenders are older men. Young women, however powerful sexually, do not normally want to exercise their powers to gain large numbers of partners . . . The anthropologists tell us that there has never been any group of women who have long permitted a regimen of group sex. Group sex has occurred chiefly when powerful men have enforced it. Any sexual revolution, therefore, will tend to liberate more men than women. Larger numbers of men than women will command two or more exclusive partners. Thus a sexual revolution will

exclude many more young men than young women... Sexual liberals and revolutionaries are anything but egalitarians. They are just men with sexual ambition or dreams of orgiastic glory. What happens when sex is liberated is not equality but a vast intensification of sexual competition, from which there is no sure haven except impotence and defeat; competition in which marriage is just another arena, or the home base from which the strong deploy; competition in which the only sure result is an ever larger band of vindictive losers... That most people can live with sexual "liberation" may in some sense be true. But what is also true, and more to the point, is that such "liberation" makes criminals out of many men and deprives even larger numbers of men and women alike of the essentials of human dignity and love.[39]

A social structure based on marriage is probably the only way for real sex freedom to develop. Dr. Fred Feldman, of the University of Southern California, explains:

Sex is the only situation in which people can express full, mutual trust. They express this to each other. Free expression in sex demands complete trust, for the individual is fully revealed as a person. He reveals his personality more completely, more intimately, in the sex relationship than in any other form of human behavior. The true sex freedom is achieved when one has sufficient trust in the partner to reveal him/herself without inhibitions. Such trust is possible only in marriage and develops with the growth of love.[40]

The idea that one could be "freer" and less inhibited with a stranger merely means one could be less inhibited with someone never to be seen again, which in turn means thinking your true self is something to be hidden. That's not sexual or any other kind of "freedom."

The gospel is the good news of freedom. It proclaims that you are loved, no matter what. You are totally loved by God. Since you have his love, and therefore do not *have* to have the affirmation and acceptance of others, you are free to affirm and accept them. The Christian is free to love just because he does not have to love.

Psychiatrists and marriage counselors have often helped people claim a share of life and happiness. Some have also said at times that there is nothing sacred about particular sexual regulations or about marriage vows. But because a person experiences emancipation from the law he has known, he may think he is free. But in fact he exchanges one law for another. The new laws may be uninhibitedness, spontaneity, self-assertion, doing what one really wants to do rather than what he thinks he *ought* to do. You give up the old ideals of self-sacrifice and resignation in exchange for the new law of self-realization and spontaneity.

The good news of the Gospel is not contained in either the old laws or the new ones.

> The good news is *neither* that you should sacrifice yourself *nor* that you should fulfill yourself. The good news is that you don't have to do either one. You are free to adopt either the ideal of self-sacrifice or the ideal of self-realization, or both, or neither, or some combination — not according to your fancy, but according to merits you percieve in them.[41]

You must decide what to do in any given situation based on your answer to the question, "What is the loving thing to do?" This is the true freedom of the Christian person who has received the good news. It is a terrifying responsibility. It frightens most people away. No wonder that when most people talk about freedom they are really referring to some newfound slavery. It is easier that way. Sexual freedom that is not used for serious expression of a profound love is the new (and old) slavery. Marriage demands and promises "gracefulness," that paradox of discipline and freedom: the discipline being the struggle to determine what is loving, and the freedom to love since we have been loved. To train us in "gracefulness," which is the shape and life of all great human achievements, is the purpose of marriage.

Adultery

In a magazine article in 1974, John H. Snow mentions a study (which at that time had not been published) of egalitarian marriages which seemed to indicate that marriage is a pretty flexible institution. Almost any division of labor can be contracted into it and survive. But the one thing that no marriage can take for long is adultery contracted into it with the mutual consent of both parties. Eventually, the angers aroused blow the marriage sky high.[42] I think the reason this is so comes from the unexamined ideals with which people try to glorify adultery. They think it is "human," "free" and "loving." Let us look at these ideals:

To be human. What does this mean? Too often, people mean by this the acceptance of the complexity of their human nature with its contradictory impulses, its inconsistencies, its mysteries. But to be human also means to engage in a struggle for unity, wholeness, and order within the complexities of personality. To be fully human is to add will and purpose and meaning to "doin' what comes naturally." A human being is designed to be "more" than what he just naturally is. To reflect God is the purpose of being human. Jesus Christ did this perfectly. He was the most "human" of us all.

To be free. Freedom is merely the context out of which value can come. As Albert Camus has said, "Freedom is nothing else but a chance to be better."[43] Value is created by the choices we make. There are really two levels of freedom. The first makes it possible for us to choose. The second is the result of the choices we make. If we choose the good, we enjoy the freedom which comes from right relationships. If we make bad choices, we forfeit the higher freedom and become embroiled in evil. Jesus was the most free man because, in his first level of freedom, all his choices were for the good, which resulted in his enjoying to the fullest that second level of freedom. He called it "the kingdom of heaven."

To be loving. Love is generally thought of as a one hundred percent good thing. Sometimes to say an act is loving can be to remove it from further analysis. Certainly, it is better to make mistakes in the name of love than in any other name, but still, the practical implementation of love demands struggle in every particular case. What is the most loving thing for this particular person in this particular situation? This is always an infinitely complex question. To "do good" for anyone else demands that you know, or at least work at trying to know, everything possible about that person so that you can know most practically what is the "good" for him or her. Jesus was the most loving person because he knew more than anyone else what were the deepest needs of those he loved.

Adultery is not human, it is not free, and it is not loving. And it also does not work. As Bach and Wyden wisely say in their book, *The Intimate Enemy:*

> Initially, . . . affairs provide an intriguing change of pace in the accustomed sex life of intimates. But the fun only lingers if the lovers manage to focus exclusively on sexy-sex. Unfortunately, [I would say "fortunately," for our humanity] affairs never seem to stay that way. The hunger for deeper intimacy reaches out beyond lusty physical sex. Good lovers nearly always tend to get more totally involved. Their playmates become helpmates. Then the lover becomes, in effect, a second wife or husband and the love affair turns into an additional intimate system with problems similar to those faced by the married partners.[44]

To be human at its highest is to be integrated, to "have it all together," for the purpose of giving that integrated self to another self. To give oneself sexually to more than one person is to act out the old disunity within.

Freedom is given us as a context out of which we do the opposite — commit ourselves. To use freedom to commit ourselves less than totally to more than one person is to misuse freedom by hanging on to it as an end rather than a means. To love is to work at understanding the needs of another toward their highest fulfillment and to act in such a way as to attempt to meet those needs. This is such a deep, complex and endless process that it would not seem possible for one person to fully commit himself to do this for more than one other person. The two become one flesh. In that one flesh is more than enough reality for two. In that unity we most surely discover our humanity, feel a new level of freedom, and know the demands and delights of love.

Fidelity

Life is full of demands for fidelity. We are continually putting ourselves in the hands of others. Human life could not go on if it were otherwise. We are always having to trust people. And along with this trust comes the demand that the one we trust be trustworthy, faithful, to us. This is the bedrock of human society, and it reflects the way ultimate reality is. God is the faithful Father we can always count on. Reality is trustable. That is the reason we believe that when someone is "true," meaning in congruence with reality, he can be relied upon; he can be trusted; he is faithful. Thus, the inner characteristic of God himself becomes known through the fidelity of another. If God loves man with faithful love, then it is fitting that children be nurtured in a social structure that is designed to show forth in a practical way God's love for people and the fidelity required in man's responding love. The way we love each other in our families is the way we make these ultimate truths concrete. Monotheism has its natural reflection in monogamy. As G.K. Chesterton once said,

> One sun is splendid; six suns would be only vulgar. One tower of Giotto is sublime; a row of towers of Giotto would be only like a row of white posts. The poetry of art is in beholding a single tower; the poetry of nature in seeing the single tree; the poetry of love in following the single woman; the poetry of religion in following the single star.[45]

True fidelity is active and creative. It is loving the other not just for what he or she is at the moment, but for what the person can become in the future. Fidelity is a lot like faith. It believes that what any marriage is in its fullness has yet to be revealed. God loves us this way: his love for us as we are enables us to become what he knows we can be. In the same way, conjugal fidelity is faith in the promise of what the marriage will be. And in the security of that faithful love the miracle of increasing "oneness" can take place. The gift of love is always the gift of time. Love "promises" in the sense that it guarantees love not only for "now" but also for the future. It pledges to give along with love the time necessary for its growth and fulfillment. The greatest love is faithful and projects that faithfulness into all the time there is.

AFTERWORD

Someone has said that there are two kinds of people, those who are interested in sex and those who are liars. You are certainly not in the latter group if you have completed this study.

I hope that each of these chapters was not only read, but also discussed in a small group. In that context, all the theories have to confront the experiential knowledge of sexuality that is found only in individuals. It is in the tension between general theories and personal experience that the truth will be found.

But there is also a wider context in which that search can be most creatively done: the religious. Religion is about right relationships between God and other persons, which is another way of describing love. Human sexuality is the structure which makes possible the most profound loving relationships. Religion helps us know what a truly loving relationship is. God is the original lover.

We humans need to be greatly loved (and only God can do that for us) so that we can become lovers. Our religious life is directly linked to our sexual lives. They are both mysteries that help us understand and live with the mystery that is each one of us. You are a unique human soul that God loves and has united with an equally unique human body, so that you can be a lover and partake in the ongoing mystery of his Kingdom coming on earth as it is in heaven.

FOOTNOTES

1. HISTORICAL BACKGROUND

1. William Graham Cole, *Sex in Christianity and Psychoanalysis* (New York: Oxford University Press, 1955), p. 5.
2. Bernard I. Murstein, *Love, Sex and Marriage Through the Ages* (New York, Springer Publishing Company, 1974), pp. 64-66.
3. *Ibid.,* p. 66.
4. Helmut Thielicke, *The Ethics of Sex,* trans. by John W. Doberstein (New York: Harper and Row, Publishers, 1964), p. 134.
5. Murstein, *Op. cit.,* pp. 113-114.
6. Cole, *Op. cit.,* pp. 88-90.
7. Derrick Sherwin Bailey, *Sexual Relation in Christian Thought* (New York: Harper and Brothers, Publishers, 1959), p. 162.
8. Paul K. Jewett, *Man as Male and Female* (Grand Rapids, Michigan: William B. Eerdmans Publishing Co., 1976), p. 155.
9. *Ibid.,* p. 158.
10. *Ibid.*
11. Herbert W. Richardson, *Nun, Witch, Playmate: The Americanization of Sex* (New York: Harper and Row, Publishers, 1971), p. 62.
12. *Ibid.,* pp. 49-55.
13. Susanne Lilar, *Aspects of Love in Western Society,* trans. by Jonathan Griffin (New York: McGraw-Hill Book Company, Inc., 1965), pp. 108-109.
14. Murstein, *Op. cit.,* p. 178.
15. William E. Phipps, *The Sexuality of Jesus* (New York: Harper and Row, Publishers, 1973), p. 103.
16. Murstein, *Op. cit.,* p. 179.
17. *Ibid.,* p. 199.
18. *Ibid.,* pp. 245-247.
19. *Ibid.,* pp. 288-289.
20. E. Jones, *The Life and Work of Sigmund Freud, Volume 1: The Formative Years and Great Discoveries, 1856-1900* (New York: Basic Books, 1953), pp. 176-177.
21. Philip Rieff, *Freud: The Mind of the Moralist* (Garden City, New York: Viking Press, Inc., 1961), p. 180.
22. Sigmund Freud, *Three Essays on Sexuality (1905),* as quoted in Reiff, *Op. cit.,* p. 181.
23. *Ibid.,* p. 183.
24. Murstein, *Op. cit.,* p. 295.
25. *Ibid.*

2. BIBLICAL BACKGROUND

1. Eugene Maly, "Human Sexuality and the Scriptures," *A Biblical and*

Dogmatic Consideration of Human Sexuality (California, San Rafael: The Institute for Theological Encounter with Science and Technology, 1976), p. 44.
2. O. J. Baab, "Sex, Sexual Behavior," *Interpreter's Dictionary of the Bible* (Nashville, Tennessee: Abingdon Press), Vol. 3, 1962 ed., p. 296.
3. Stuart Barton Babbage, *Sex and Sanity: A Christian View of Sexual Morality, A Volume of Christian Foundations,* Edited by Philip E. Hughes (Philadelphia: The Westminster Press, 1965), p. 18.
4. *Ibid.*, p. 19.
5. Millar Burrows, *An Outline of Biblical Theology* (Philadelphia: The Westminster Press, 1946), p. 297.
6. R. Franklin Terry, "Religion and Sexuality in John Updike's *A Month of Sundays,*" *Anglican Theological Review,* Vol. LIX, No. 1, January, 1977, p. 59.
7. Burrows, *Op. cit.*, p. 297.
8. William E. Phipps, *The Sexuality of Jesus* (New York: Harper and Row, 1973), p. 148.
9. Derrick Sherwin Bailey, *Sexual Relation in Christian Thought* (New York: Harper and Brothers Publishers, 1959), p. 10.
10. L. H. Marshall, *The Challenge of New Testament Ethics* (London: Macmillan and Company, Ltd., 1950), p. 36.
11. C. F. D. Moule, *The Phenomenon of the New Testament, Studies in Biblical Theology,* Second Series, No. 1 (Naperville, Illinois: Alec R. Allenson, Inc., 1967. Excerpts reprinted by permission.), p. 63.
12. *Ibid.*, p. 65.
13. Joachim Kahl, *The Misery of Christianity,* Translated by N. D. Smith (Harmondsworth, England: Penguin Books, Ltd., 1972), p. 74.
14. Phipps, *Op. cit.*, p. 60
15. *Ibid.*, p. 68.
16. Paul K. Jewett, *Man as Male and Female,* (Grand Rapids, Michigan: William B. Eerdmans Publishing Co., 1976), p. 106.
17. Tom F. Driver, "Sexuality and Jesus," *New Theology,* No. 3, Martin E. Marty and Dean G. Peerman, eds. (New York: The Macmillan Co., 1966) pp. 129-130. Reprinted by permission of the author and his agent, James Brown Asociates, Inc., © 1965, by Union Theological Seminary in the city of New York.
18. William R. Hoyt, *Christian Century,* 1971, as quoted in Phipps, *Op. cit.,* p. 147.
19. Phipps, *Op. cit.*, p. 150.
20. Karl Kraus, *Auswahl aus dem Werk,* as quoted in Adolf Holl, *Jesus in Bad Company* Translated by Simon King (New York: Holt, Reinhart, and Winston, 1971), pp. 78, 79.

3. COMTEMPORARY THEORIES OF SEXUALITY

1. Albert Ellis, *Sex Without Guilt,* as quoted in James R. Smith and Lynn J. Smith, eds., *Beyond Monogamy* (Baltimore: The Johns Hopkins

University Press, 1974), p. 23.
2. William H. Masters and Virginia E. Johnson, *The Pleasure Bond* (Boston: Little, Brown, and Company, 1974), p. 254.
3. Philip Rieff, *Freud: The Mind of the Moralist* (Garden City, New York: Viking Press, Inc., 1961), p. 356.
4. Prescott Lecky, *Self-consistency* as cited in Calvin S. Hall and Gardner Lindsey, *Theories of Personality* (New York: John Wiley and Sons, Inc., 1970), p. 329.
5. Peter Berger, "Cakes for the Queen of Heaven: 2,500 Years of Religious Ecstacy," *Christian Century*, December 25, 1974, p. 1218.
6. Daniel Day Williams, *The Spirit and the Forms of Love* (New York: Harper and Row, Publishers, 1968), p. 232.
7. D. H. Lawrence, as quoted in Charles Fair, *The New Nonsense — The End of the Rational Consensus*, (New York: Simon and Schuster, 1974), p. 195.
8. Norman Mailer, as quoted in E. LaB. Cherbonnier, *Hardness of Heart* (Garden City, New York: Doubleday and Company, 1955), p. 175.
9. Dorothea Krook, as quoted in Daniel Day Williams, *The Spirit and the Forms of Love* (New York: Harper and Row, Publishers, 1968), p. 233. Reprinted by permission.
10. Rollo May, *Love and Will* (New York: W. W. Norton and Company, Inc., 1969), p. 91.
11. Eric Fromm, referred to in Institute for Theological Encounter with Science and Technology, *A Biblical and Dogmatic Consideration of Human Sexuality* (San Rafael, California: n.p., 1976), p. 60.
12. Derrick Sherwin Bailey, *Sexual Relation in Christian Thought* (New York: Harper and Brothers, Publishers, 1959), pp. 281-282.
13. *Ibid.*, p. 282.
14. Ernest Becker, *The Denial of Death* (New York: The Free Press, 1973), p. 162. Reprinted by permission.
15. *Ibid.*, p. 163.
16. *Ibid.*, p. 167.
17. Irving Singer, *The Goals of American Sexuality* (New York: Schocken Books, 1974), p. 43.
18. Robert T. Francoeur, *Eve's New Rib — Twenty Faces of Sex, Marriage, and Family*, (New York: Dell Publishing Company, 1973), p. 40.
19. Irving Singer, *Op. cit.*, p. 48.
20. Stendhal as quoted in Irving Singer, *Op. cit.*, p. 57.
21. John Sheets, "The Mystery of Sexuality and the Mystery of Revelation," Institute for Theological Encounter with Science and Technology, *A Biblical and Dogmatic Consideration of Human Sexuality* (San Rafael, California: n.p., 1976), p. 82.
22. *Ibid.*, p. 83.
23. Phillippe the Carmeline, as quoted in Ralph Harper, *Human Love Existential and Mystical* (Baltimore: The Johns Hopkins University Press, 1966), p. 13.
24. Martin D'Arcy, as quoted in Ralph Harper, *Op. cit.*, p. 34.
25. Reinhold Niebuhr, *The Nature and Destiny of Man* (New York:

Charles Scribner's Sons, 1949), pp. 233-234 and 236-237.
26. Nicolas Berdyaev, *Freedom and the Spirit*, translated by Oliver Fielding Clarke (London: The Centenary Press, April, 1948), p. 200.
27. Ralph Harper, *Op. cit.*, p. 69.
28. *Ibid.*, p. 70.
29. Vladimir Solovyev, *The Meaning of Love*, (New York: International University Press, 1947), p. 57.

4. MALE-FEMALE DIFFERENCES

1. John Macmurray, *Reason and Emotion*, second edition (Great Britain: Faber and Faber LTD, 1962), pp. 118-120. Reprinted by permission.
2. Sidney Cornelia Callahan, *The Illusion of Eve — Modern Woman's Quest for Identity* (New York: Sheed and Ward, 1965), p. 15.
3. Eric Fromm, *The Art of Loving*, as cited in Sidney Cornelia Callahan, *Op. cit., p. 19f.*
4. Ruth T. Barnhouse and Urban T. Holmes, III, eds., *Male and Female — Christian Approaches to Sexuality* (New York: The Seabury Press, 1976), p. 5. Reprinted by permission.
5. Sy and Gill Miller, "Open Letter to Man," *Our Sunday Visitor*, January 25, 1970, p. 10.
6. Robin Morgan, ed., *Sisterhood is Powerful* (New York: Random House, 1970), p. 557ff.
7. Joseph Zubin and John Money, eds., *Contemporary Sexual Behavior: Critical Issues in the 1970's* (Baltimore: The Johns Hopkins University Press, 1973), p. 149.
8. *Ibid.*
9. Robin Morgan, *Op. cit.*, p. 514.
10. *Ibid.*, p. 539ff.
11. Eugene C. Bianchi, "The Superbowl Culture of Male Violence, *The Christian Century*, September 18, 1974, p. 843.
12. *Ibid.* p. 842.
13. Gallup Youth Poll, as cited in the *Lawrence Daily Journal World*, Lawrence, Kansas, July 20, 1977, p. 19.
14. Theo Lang, *The Difference Between a Man and a Woman* (New York: Bantam Books, 1973), p. 212.
15. Theodore Reik, as cited in Vance Packard, *The Sexual Wilderness, The Contemporary Upheaval in Male-Female Relationships* (New York: David McKay Company, Inc., 1968), p. 118.
16. Vance Packard, *The Sexual Wilderness, The Contemporary Upheaval in Male-Female Relationships* (New York: David McKay Company, Inc., 1968), p. 122.
17. *Ibid.*, p. 126.
18. Theo Lang, *Op cit.*, p. 215.
19. Dr. Melvin Anchell, *Sex and Sanity* (New York: The Macmillan Company, 1971), p. 42f.
20. Simone de Beauvoir, *The Second Sex*, translated and edited by H. M.

Parshley (New York: Bantam Books, Inc., 1953), pp. 24-26.
21. Margaret Mead, as cited in Sidney Cornelia Callahan, *Op. Cit.,* p. 14.
22. Mary Jane Sherfey, as cited in Herbert A. Otto, ed., *The New Sexuality* (Palo Alto, California: Science and Behavior Books, Inc., 1971), p. 29.
23. Lawrence H. Fuchs, *Family Matters* (New York: Random House, 1972), p. 131. Reprinted by permission.
24. *Ibid.,* p. 132.
25. *Ibid.,* p. 133.
26. Karl Bednarik, *The Male In Crisis,* translated by Helen Sebba (New York: Alfred A. Knopf. 1970), p. 14.
27. *Ibid.,* p. 15.
28. Margaret Mead, *Male and Female,* as quoted in Valerie Saiving Goldstein, "The Human Situation: A Feminine Viewpoint," *Pastoral Psychology,* April, 1966, p. 36.
29. Eleanor Emmons Maccoby and Carol Nagy Jacklin, *The Psychology of Sex Differences* (Stanford, California: Stanford University Press, 1974).
30. *Ibid.,* p. 361.
31. *Ibid.,* p. 243.
32. Steven Goldberg, *The Inevitability of Patriarchy* (New York: William Morrow and Company, Inc., 1973), p. 32. Reprinted by permission.
33. *Ibid.,* p. 51.
34. *Ibid.,* p. 228.
35. Eleanor Emmons Maccoby and Carol Nagy Jacklin, *Op. cit.,* pp. 368-369.
36. Richard C. Friedman, Ralph M. Richart, and Raymond L. Van de Wille, eds., *Sex Differences in Behavior* (New York: John Wiley and Sons, Incorporated, 1974), p. 335.
37. Helmut Thielicke, *The Ethics of Sex,* translated by John W. Doberstein (New York: Harper and Row, Publishers, 1964), pp. 80-83. Reprinted by permission.
38. Joseph Zubin and John Money, eds., *Op. cit.,* p. 421. Reprinted by permission.
39. Kenneth Walker, as cited in Isadore Rubin, ed., *Sexual Freedom in Marriage* (New York: The New American Library, Inc., Signet Books, 1969), p. 77.
40. W. J. Kalt and R. J. Wilkins, *Man and Woman* (Chicago: Henry Regenery Company, n.d.), p. 12.
41. Theodore Lidz, *The Person — His and Her Development Throughout the Life Cyle,* revised edition (New York: Basic Books, Inc., 1976), p. 369.
42. Mary Jane Sherfey, *The Nature and Evolution of Female Sexuality* (New York: Random House, 1972), p. 138 and footnote.
43. *Ibid.,* p. 139.
44. Anne Koedt, as quoted in Midge Decter, *The New Chastity* (New York: Berkley Publishing Corporation, 1973), p. 80.
45. William H. Masters and Virginia E. Johnson, *Human Sexual Response,* as quoted in Robin Morgan, *Op. cit.,* p. 199f.
46. Seward Hiltner, "The Neglected Phenomenon of Female

Homosexuality," *Christian Century*, May 29, 1974, p. 592f. Reprinted by permission of The Christian Century Foundation.

5. PRE-MARITAL SEXUALITY

1. Robert C. Sorensen, *Adolescent Sexuality in Contemporary America, Personal Values and Sexual Behavior, Ages Thirteen to Nineteen* (New York: World Publishing, 1973).
2. Herbert A. Otto, ed., *The New Sexuality* (Palo Alto, California: Science and Behavior Books, Inc., 1971), p. 37.
3. *Sexology*, June, 1968, as quoted in Herbert A. Otto, *Op. cit.*, p. 38.
4. *Ibid.*
5. *Ibid.*, p. 39.
6. John A. T. Robinson, *The Human Face of God* (Philadelphia: The Westminster Press, 1973), p. 62. f.n.
7. *Ibid.*, p. 59.
8. William Graham Cole, *Sex in Christianity and Psychoanalysis* (New York: Oxford University Press, 1955), p. 27.
9. Rustum Roy and Della Roy, *Honest Sex, A Revolutionary New Sex Guide for the Now Generation of Christians* (New York: The New American Library, Inc., Signet Books, 1969), p. 65. Reprinted by permission.
10. Lester Kirkendall, as quoted in Joseph Fletcher, *Moral Responsibility — Situation Ethics at Work* (Philadelphia: The Westminster Press, 1967), p. 134f.
11. *Ibid.*, p. 135.
12. Lester Kirkendall, *Premarital Intercourse and Interpersonal Relations*, as quoted in Urban T. Holmes, III, *The Sexual Person — The Church's Role in Human Sexual Development* (New York: The Seabury Press, 1970), p. 19.
13. Joseph Fletcher, *Moral Responsibility — Situation Ethics at Work* (Philadelphia: The Westminster Press, 1967), p. 137.
14. Alfred North Whitehead, as quoted in Norman Pittenger, *Love and Control in Sexuality* (Philadelphia: United Church Press, 1974), p. 87.
15. Theodore Lidz, *The Person — His and Her Development Throughout the Life Cyle*, revised edition (New York: Basic Books, Inc., 1976), p. 370. Reprinted by permission.
16. *Ibid.*, p. 371.
17. Vance Packard, "Possible Elements for a Modern Sex Code," *Pastoral Psychology*, Vol. 21, No. 208 (November, 1970), p. 40.
18. *Ibid.*
19. Herbert W. Richardson, *Nun, Witch, Playmate: The Americanization of Sex* (New York: Harper and Row, Publishers, 1971), p. 15. Reprinted by Permission.
20. *Ibid.*, p. 7.
21. *Ibid.*, p. 14.
22. *Ibid.*, p. 20.
23. *Ibid.*, p. 37.

24. Ibid., p. 38.
25. Ibid., p. 41.
26. Donald R. Cutter, ed., *The Religious Situation, 1969* (Boston: The Beacon Press, 1969), p. 790.
27. Herbert W. Richardson, *Op. cit.*, p. 84.
28. Ibid., p. 85.
29. Ibid., p. 87.
30. Ibid., p. 98.
31. Ibid., p. 99.
32. Sidney Callahan, as quoted in David Darst and Joseph Forque, eds., *Sexuality on Island Earth* (New York: Paulist Press, 1970), p. 51.

6. HOMOSEXUALITY

1. Letter to the editor, *Time*, July 4, 1977, p. 4.
2. Norman Pittenger, "E. M. Forster, Homosexuality and Christian Morality," *The Christian Century*, December 15, 1971, p. 1469.
3. Robert W. Wood, *Joint Strategy and Action Committee Grapevine*, May, 1971, Vol. 2, No. 10.
4. Ibid.
5. Ibid.
6. Leon Smith, "Religion's Response to the New Sexuality," *Siecus Report*, Vol. IV, No. 2, November, 1975, p. 15.
7. Ibid.
8. *Joint Strategy and Action Committee Grapevine, Op. cit.*
9. Ibid.
10. Episcopal Church, Resolution from 1976 Convention.
11. Ruth Tiffany Barnhouse, "Homosexuality," *Anglican Theological Review, Supplementary Series*, No. 6, June, 1976, p. 110.
12. Herant A. Katchadourian, M.D., and Donald T. Lunde, M.D., *Fundamentals of Human Sexuality* (New York: Holt, Rinehart, and Winston, Inc., 1972), p. 276.
13. Ibid., p. 279.
14. Irving Singer, *The Goals of Human Sexuality* (New York: Schocken Books, 1974), p. 156.
15. Ruth Tiffany Barnhouse, as quoted in *The Living Church*, January 16, 1977, p. 6.
16. Alan P. Bell, as quoted in *Anglican Theological Review*, April, 1977, p. 189.
17. Seward Hiltner, "The Neglected Phenomenon of Female Homosexuality," *The Christian Century*, May 29, 1974, p. 591.
18. George F. Will, "How Far Out of the Closet?" *Newsweek*, May 30, 1977, p. 92.
19. Calvin S. Hall and Gardner Lindsey, *Theories of Personality* (New York: John Wiley and Sons, Inc., 1970), p. 148.
20. W. Paul Jones, "Homosexuality and Marriage: Exploring on the Theological Edge," *Pastoral Psychology*, Vol. 21, No. 209. December,

1970, p. 34. Reprinted by permission.
21. Irving Singer, *Op. cit.*, p. 157.
22. Herant A. Katchadourian and Donald T. Lunde, *Op. cit.*, pp. 266-267.
23. Norman Pittenger, "E. M. Forster, Homosexuality and Christian Morality, *The Christian Century*, December 15, 1971, p. 1470. Reprinted by permission of The Christian Century Foundation.
24. *Ibid.*
25. W. Paul Jones, *Op. cit.*, pp. 29-37. Reprinted by permission.
26. George F. Will, *Op. cit.*, p. 92.
27. Ruth Tiffany Barnhouse, *Anglican Theological Review*, *Op. cit.*, p. 129f. Reprinted by permission.

7. MARRIAGE

1. Nena O'Neill, *The Marriage Premise* (New York: M. Evans and Company, Incorporated, 1977).
2. Nena O'Neill and George O'Neill, *Open Marriage: A New Life Style for Couples* (New York: M. Evans and Company, Incorporated, 1972), p. 246. Reprinted by permission of the publisher.
3. James R. Smith and Lynn G. Smith, eds., *Beyond Monogamy* (Baltimore: The Johns Hopkins University Press, 1974), p. 21.
4. *Ibid.*, p. 19. Reprinted by permission.
5. Ronald Mazur, *The New Intimacy — Open Ended Marriage and Alternative Lifestyles* (Boston: Beacon Press, 1973), p. 12. Excerpts reprinted by permission.
6. *Ibid.*, p. 13.
7. James R. Smith and Lynn G. Smith, eds., *Op. cit.*, p. 33.
8. Ronald Mazur, *Op. cit.*, p. 14.
9. *Ibid.*, p. 17.
10. James R. Smith and Lynn G. Smith, eds., *Op. cit.*, pp. 62-63.
11. *Ibid.*, p. 62.
12. Nena O'Neill and George O'Neill, *Op. cit.*, p. 256. Reprinted by permission of the publisher.
13. Alastair Heron, ed., *Towards a Quaker View of Sex* (London: Friends Home Service Committee, 1963), p. 45.
14. Rustum Roy and Della Roy, *Honest Sex: A Revolutionary New Sex Guide for the Now Generation of Christians* (New York: The New American Library, Incorporated, Signet Books, 1969), p. 121. Excerpts reprinted by permission.
15. *Ibid.*, p. 112.
16. *Ibid.*, p. 114.
17. *Ibid.*, p. 121.
18. William H. Masters and Virginia E. Johnson, *The Pleasure Bond* (Boston: Little, Brown and Company and Bantam Books, Inc., 1975), p. 184. By permission of Bantam Books, Inc. All rights reserved.
19. O.S. English, ed., *The New Sexuality* (Palo Alto, California: Science and Behavior Books, Incorporated, 1971), p. 192.

20. Edmund L. Van Deusen, *Contract Cohabitation: An Alternative to Marriage* (New York: Grove Press, Incorporated, 1974), p. 12.
21. *Ibid.*, pp. 14-15.
22. *Ibid.*, pp. 44-45.
23. *Ibid.*, p. 20.
24. *Ibid.*, p. 80.
25. *U. S. News and World Reports*, July 25, 1977, p. 76.
26. Anna K. Francoeur and Robert T. Francoeur, *Hot and Cool Sex — Cultures in Conflict* (New York: Harcourt, Brace and Jovanovich, 1974), p. 69.
27. Philip Rieff, *The Triumph of the Therapeutic. Uses of Faith After Freud* (New York: Harper and Row, Publishers, 1966), p. 219.
28. William H. Masters and Virginia E. Johnson, *Op. cit.*, p. 140.
29. James R. Smith and Lynn G. Smith, eds., *Op. cit.*, pp. 31-32.
30. William H. Masters and Virginia E. Johnson, *Op. cit.*, p. 144.
31. *Ibid.*, p. 143.
32. *Ibid.*, p. 145.
33. Ronald Mazur, *Op. cit.*, p. 58.
34. William F. Rollo, *A Catalog of Sins* (New York: Holt, Rinehart and Winston, 1967), p. 130.
35. Werner Pelz and Lottie Pelz, *God is No More* (Philadelphia: J. B. Lippincott company, 1963), p. 42.
36. George Gilder, *Sexual Suicide* (New York: Bantan Books, 1975), p. 1.
37. Reprinted by permission of Times Books, a division of Quadrangle/The New York Times Book Co. Inc., from *Naked Nomads* by George Gilder, copyright © 1974 by George F. Gilder; and from *Sexual Suicide* by George F. Gilder, copyright © 1973 by George F. Gilder.
38. *Ibid.*
39. *Ibid.*, p. 36.
40. Fred Feldman, as quoted in Howard Whitman, *The Sex Age* (New York: Charter Books, 1963), p. 231.
41. John Cobb, "Justification by Faith," a sermon in *Master Sermon Series* (Detroit: Cathedral Publishers, August, 1970), p. 481.
42. John H. Snow, "On the Other Hand," *The Witness*, October 13, 1974, Vol. 58, No. 1, p. 7.
43. Lawrence J. Peter, *Peter's Quotations* (New York: William Morrow and Company, Incorporated, 1977), p. 209.
44. George R. Bach and Peter Wyden, *The Intimate Enemy — How to Fight Fair in Love and Marriage* (New York: William Morrow and Company, Incorporated, 1969), p. 245.
45. G. K. Chesterton, as quoted in C. L. Wallis, *A Treasury of Sermon Illustrations* (New York and Nashville: Abingdon-Cokesbury Press, 1950), p. 224.